Learn Hebrew In
7 DAYS!

The Ultimate Crash Course to Learning the Basics of the Hebrew Language in No Time

By Dagny Taggart

Disclaimer

The information provided in this book is designed to provide helpful information on the subjects discussed. The author's books are only meant to provide the reader with the basics knowledge of a certain language, without any warranties regarding whether the student will, or will not, be able to incorporate and apply all the information provided. Although the writer will make her best effort share her insights, language learning is a difficult task, and each person needs a different timeframe to fully incorporate a new language. This book, nor any of the author's books constitute a promise that the reader will learn a certain language within a certain timeframe.

Table of Contents

Dedicated to those who love going beyond their own frontiers.

Keep on traveling,

Dagny Taggart

Introduction
Are You Ready for an Amazing Journey?

Most people are daunted by the idea of learning a language. They think it's impossible, even unfathomable. I remember growing up with Israelis constantly visiting my parents and not understanding a world of what was going on around me. I remember my parents switching languages and being surprised that they spoke two languages.

I tried teaching myself a couple of different languages without much success. In 4th and 5th grade, I tried to learn Chinese. It didn't work out so well because I didn't know that Chinese was tonal and that you actually need practice to learn a language. However, since then I've learned to speak Hebrew and Arabic and will be tackling French or Spanish in the near future. It is possible to learn a foreign language, millions of people around the world speak two or three languages fluently. All it takes to learn a second or even third language is to be willing to make mistakes and put in the time to practice!

This book will only provide the basics in order to start learning Hebrew. It is designed for those who plan on visiting Israel. It will cover the scenarios you are most likely to end up in. Feel free to skip to what you feel is relevant.

Important note

Due to the nature of this book (it contains charts, graphs, and so on), you will better your reading experience by setting your device on *LANDSCAPE* mode!

Language Tips

Tip #1 - Keep an Open Mind

It should be obvious but it is important you understand that languages may be completely different from each other. You can't expect what you say in English to be the same in Hebrew. So, try to get used to translating complete ideas. This way Hebrew grammar won't be completely backwards to you. Keep an open mind and be aware of the differences in Hebrew that include words, sentences and even sounds.

Tip #2 - Take Risks

Don't be scared to talk to people.   Practice makes perfect and it's true for languages.   Don't be embarrassed for mixing up the pronouns for *he* and *she* or say "fish" rather than "dog", which are common mistakes.   Learn from the mistakes and move on.

Tip #3 - Learn from your Mistakes

Don't get depressed over one mistake while trying to take a taxi or ordering food at the neighborhood Shwarma joint.   Making mistakes is a HUGE part of learning a language. You have to put yourself out there and be willing to make tons of mistakes! Why? Because you can LEARN from them.   Not making a mistake probably means you're not learning what you could.   In a language like Hebrew, you will make mistakes.   Even native Israelis make mistakes!   So every time you mess up when trying to communicate, learn from it, move on, and keep your head up!

Tip #4 - Immerse yourself in the language

If you are unable to goto Israel, you still have numerous tools you can use to surround yourself with the language.   Listen to Israeli music, watch TV shows and movies that are in Hebrew.   You can even switch your computer, phone, mp3 player or any other electronics to Hebrew.   You will have to relearn these devices, but it will help in the long run.   I strongly recommend this.   Reading Hebrew newspapers and listening to Israeli radio dramatically improved your Hebrew.   In fact, if you can passively listen to the Israeli news board bast on the radio without having to think, your Hebrew is more than fluent - you can consider yourself Israeli!

Tip #5 - Start Thinking in Hebrew

In college, when I started learning Arabic, I used to occasionally think to myself in Arabic when I was running around the track.   You can do this too with Hebrew.   Describe your surroundings wherever you are, what you did that day of the week and what else you have to do before the end of the week.   When you're not doing anything important - or even when doing something important - try thinking in Hebrew!

Tip #6 - Label your Surroundings/Use Flashcards

A great way to learn a language quickly is to label rooms, appliances and other items with tags in Hebrew. This will help you build vocabulary quickly.   My mother did this when she was taking a brush-up course on Hebrew.   It drove us crazy because there were stickers all over the place, but everyone at home learned to say a wide range of words in Hebrew!   I recommend doing this once you have learned verb forms and conjugations -just write down the charts and memorize!   You can also do this with any other language that you may want to learn in the future!

Tip #7 - Use Context clues, visuals, gestures, expressions, etc.

If you don't understand a word you heard or read, try to figure out the context as a clue.   If you are in a store and your friend says, "I am going to _____ a felafel", you can safely guess she said *order* or *eat* but you don't have to understand every word in order to get the gist of what was said. When you are in a conversation use gestures, expressions, and things around you to help communicate.   Be willing to act things out.   It may look silly, but you will learn languages much faster if you can act out the word you're looking for.

Tip #8 - Circumlocution

Circumlo... what? This is a fancy word for describing something when you don't know how to say it.   If you are looking to buy a pair of sandals and don't know how to say it, you can describe sandals using words you know.   You can say it's worn in the summer on the feet, it has straps on it.   Hopefully someone will understand what you mean and give you right word.   Circumlocution is also excellent language practice - you'll be speaking the language more while trying to describe what it is you want!

Tip #9 - Pay Attention to Patterns!

Hebrew is based on a triconsonantal root system.   This means that almost every single word in the language can be traced to a three letter root.   Use this to your advantage because once you you learn one word, you can learn another 10-15 related words just by putting the root into different verb and noun patterns.   Paying attention to patterns will make it easy to understand words and build your vocabulary quickly!

SECTION 1
THE BASICS

Chapter 1
Why You Can't Afford Not to Learn Hebrew (Yes, I'm Serious!)

You've decided to learn Hebrew! Congratulations! Thousands of people have taken the path you are embarking on now and I'm not just talking about immigrants to Israel and Jews around the world.   No, I mean people just like you who want to learn another language.   However, if you're not convinced you should learn Hebrew, here are some reasons why you should learn Hebrew.

1) Hebrew is the language of the Bible.   If you are a religious person and would like to know what the Bible says in its original language, you need to learn Hebrew.   Hebrew is the language the Bible was composed in.   In addition, if you're interested in Judaism, the religious texts are mostly written in Hebrew.   If you understand Hebrew, you can study Jewish religious texts and gain an understanding of Judaism.

2)   You want to visit Israel.   While Israelis speak other languages such as English and French, it's easy to get lost in Israel if you don't speak Hebrew. This is especially in out-of-the-way places.   I can think of a few places where it was really good that I spoke Hebrew because I could have gotten really lost and misunderstood people.

3) If you learn Hebrew, you can learn other languages in the Semitic language family.   All languages in the Semitic language family are closely related, with words in the different languages sounding vaguely similar and even identical with same meaning.   If you learn Hebrew, one of the more complicated languages in the family because of Jewish history and the influence of outside languages such as German, you can easily pick up Arabic.

4)   You have relatives in Israel.   You'll be able to communicate with your relatives more easily.   This is certainly the case if you plan on staying with those relatives for any extended period of time.

5) Understanding Hebrew will help with understand Middle East politics. Let's face it, what goes on in the Middle East catches everyones attention and interest.   However, there is often a one-dimensional portrayal of what happens in the region.   The lack of knowledge of the local languages by the media means that news is reported in an inaccurate and often highly biased manner, in both directions.   If you learn Hebrew, you can gain a certain understanding of at least one of the view points of Middle Eastern politics, that of Israel. This is a good thing because Israelis have a wide range of views on different topics, some of which can be eyebrow-raising and way outside the box.

6)   You want to understand what goes on synagogues.   In Judaism, the prayers are recited in Hebrew.   While many books have translations, there is nothing like the original language.   Consequently, learning Hebrew is essential if you want to understand the prayers and what is being said.

7)   Academic research.   If you are an academic and one that focuses on philosophy, theology or another other field where Jews had a major contribution, you will want to know Hebrew.   This is because Jews by and large wrote in Hebrew throughout history even though they also composed works in other languages as well.   There are math treatises written completely in Hebrew, for one example.

Chapter 2
Getting the Pronunciation Down

Below I will break down general Israeli Hebrew pronunciation for the whole alphabet dividing it into vowels and consonants. Hebrew letters stay the same with the sound they make, although vowels can sometimes be complicated. Vowels also are marked by a series of dots and lines beneath the letters, although they almost never appear in written text. Hebrew also has a much smaller set of sounds so it is easier to learn the sounds! There are some sounds in Hebrew that do not exist in English. Don't be intimidated by the fact that Hebrew has a completely different alphabet from English - many languages do! Also, don't worry about the markings - as you learn the language, the vowel markings will become unnecessary. So get ready to start moving your mouth and tongue in a new way that may seem strange at first but will be come natural as you get used to Hebrew!

The charts on the next page will explain how to say the letter, pronounce it, and if there is an example in an English word of how to say it I put it in the right column.

NOTE: I have included the Hebrew alphabet so you can learn to recognize letters and words. I also include Hebrew spellings of words with transliterated spelling in later chapters so you can learn to read the word in Hebrew. Note that some Hebrew letters have a different form when they occur at the end of a word. I highly recommend learning to read the word in Hebrew letters rather than using the English transcription. This will make more complicated concepts such as verb conjugations and the three-letter-root system much simpler to understand.

Vowel Sounds

Vowel	Hebrew Marking	Name of Vowel	How to say the letter	How to pronounce it in a word	As in...

a		Kamatz	a	a	P<u>aw</u> (In Israel it sounds more like P<u>a</u>)
ah		Patach	ah	ah	F<u>a</u>ther
e		Segol	eh	eh	Y<u>e</u>s
ey		Tsere	ey	ey	H<u>ey</u>
u		Shuruk	oo	oo	
i		Chirik	ee/i	ee/i	B<u>ee</u>
		Shva Nach	Silent	Silent	**This is used to mark a closed syllable**
		Shva Na	This is the Schwa	uh	L<u>u</u>g
o		Cholam (this appears as a dot above a word or above a letter Vav	o	o	B<u>oa</u>t

Note: In Israel, the vowel markers are almost never used.   To get you used to this, I won't be using any of these symbols.   You should just know they appear and what sounds they correspond to.   If you would like to see how the vowels appear, I suggest using a Hebrew dictionary and look up the different vocabulary words in the book.

Consonant Sounds

Consonant	Hebrew Letter	How to say the letter	How to pronounce it in a word	As in...
a	א	Aleph	Depends on vowels, usually a	<u>a</u>h
b	ב	Bet	B or V depending on the presence of a dot in the center	<u>B</u>ow <u>V</u>iolin
g	ג	Gimmel	G	<u>G</u>o
d	ד	Daled	D	<u>D</u>og
h	ה	Heh	H	<u>H</u>at
v	ו	Vav	V (This is also sometimes used with a Cholam used to mark the O and U vowels)	<u>V</u>iolin
z	ז	Zayin	Z	<u>Z</u>ipper
h	ח	Het	Kh	Ble<u>ch</u>
t	ט	Tet	T	<u>T</u>oe

y	י	Yud	Y	<u>Y</u>es
k	כ, ך	Kaf	K or KH depending on the presence of a dot in the center of the letter	<u>K</u>ite Ble<u>ch</u>
l	ל	Lamed	L	<u>L</u>ike
m	מ ם	Mem	M	<u>m</u>oney
n	נ ן	Nun	N	<u>n</u>o
s	ס	Samech	S	<u>S</u>mile
a	ע	Ayin	an a from the back of the throat or just a (this does not exist in English and has no equivalent)	
p	פ ף	Peh	P or F, depending on the presence of a dot in the center	<u>P</u>lant <u>F</u>lower
ts/tz	צ	Tsadee	double z in Pizza	Pi<u>zz</u>a
q	ק	Kuf	K	<u>K</u>ing
r	ר	Resh	R or the French R	<u>R</u>oad <u>R</u>ouge (French)

s or sh	שׁ	Shin/Sin	S or Sh depending on the location of the dot above the letter	<u>S</u>it <u>Sh</u>ave
t	ת	Tav	T	<u>T</u>iny

Note: If you're not sure   how to pronounce a word,   one thing you can do is type it in *Google translate* then click on the little speaker icon in the bottom left corner to hear the correct pronunciation.

Chapter 3
Hebrew and English differences and Basic Grammar

We will now start with the essentials of Hebrew grammar.   I'll explain some of the major differences between Hebrew and English together with some important Hebrew grammar rules.   After that, I'll give you some vocabulary words.   The vocabulary will include question words, numbers, colors, and other useful words and phrases.   If you should forget how to say a word while working on later chapters, you'll probably find it here.

Differences between English and Hebrew

1.   **Masculine and Feminine Words:** In Hebrew there are words that are feminine and masculine. It has nothing to do with the actual word. In addition, many words that are feminine do not follow the pattern for feminine words. The same is true for masculine words.   If this is confusing, that's okay. Consider the number of exceptions to rules in English and this should seem less daunting.

2. **Word Order:** The word order is often changed. For example, the adjective goes after the noun. Instead of *blue box*, it is the *box blue* (Kufsah Kechulah)(קופסה כחולה).   The word order goes beyond this, with some statements sounding as if they are from the Biblical era.   That's because modern Hebrew, while largely based on German and thus similar to English, it still has some forms from Biblical Hebrew.   Thus while English is an SVO (Subject-Verb-Object) languages, Hebrew is both SVO and VSO (Verb-Subject-Object) language.   If   you are interested in this, I recommend looking for some academic books on the history of Hebrew.   You may also look at the website of the Academy of the Hebrew Language that creates new words and decides what is acceptable usage.   The academy's website will have plenty of information about the Hebrew language

3. **Adjective and Noun Agreement:** The adjectives must agree with the gender (feminine or masculine) and the number (singular or plural). For example, the red cars (Ha-HaMichoniyot HaAdumot)(המכוניות האדומות) or the black cat (HeChatul HaShachor)(החתול השחור)

4. **Verb Changes**:   Hebrew has more verb changes than English.   This is because of the fact that Hebrew uses patterns and its three letter root system to add aspect to verbs as well as tense.   For example, to run has four different appearances in the present tense: I run (Ani Ratz)(אני רץ) she runs (Hee Ratza)(היא רצה) we run (Anachnu Ratzim)(אנחנו רצים) they (feminine plural) run (Hen Ratzot)(הן רצות).   This becomes more complicated when you add past and future tenses.

5. **Lack of Pronoun (I, he, she, we, it, they, etc.) Use:**   Because of the verb changes mentioned in number 4, personal pronouns aren't always necessary. Instead of saying *Ani   Agi-ah*,(I will arrive)(אני אגיע) you can just say *Agi'ah* (אגיע) because we already know that is you who we are talking about from the verb.   However, you can use the pronouns, especially if you aren't familiar with the Hebrew conjugation system.

Basic Grammar

There is one way to say *the* in Hebrew.   Masculine and Feminine is completely irrelevant.

Hebrew Articles

The	Masculine	Feminine
Singular	Ha (הַ)	Ha (הַ)
Plural	Ha (הַ)	Ha (הַ)

Note: The term "Ha" appears in Hebrew as a simple letter Hey attached to the front of the word.   Note that the vowel beneath the letter can sometimes change.

 Ex: *He*Chatul ---> the cat (החתול)

*Ha*Yalda ---> the girl (הילדה)

*Ha*Klavim ---> the dogs (הכלבים)

*Ha*Agvaniot ---> the tomatoes (העגבניות)

Personal Pronouns

I	Ani (אֲנִי)
you	Ata (אתה) (Masculine) At (את) (Feminine)
He, She	Hu (הוא) Hee (היא)
We	Anachnu (אנחנו)
You (Plural)	Atem (אתם) (Masculine) Aten (אתן) (Feminine)
They/Them	Hem (הם) (Masculine) Hen (הן) (Feminine)

*As mentioned before, personal pronouns are not used as much in Hebrew

Question Words

What?	Mah? (מה)
Where?	Eyfo? (איפה)
When?	Matai? (מתי)
Which?	Eyzeh? (איזה)
Why?	Lama? (למה)
Who?	Me? (מי)

Numbers 1-10

Numbers have masculine and feminine forms.   In spoken Hebrew, the feminine form is often used in place of the masculine form.   In written Hebrew and during news broadcasts, the form below is used.

Number	Masculine Form	Feminine Form
1	Echad (אחד)	Achat (אחת)
2	Shnaim (שנים)	Shtaim (שתים)
3	Shlosha (שלושה)	Shalosh (שלוש)
4	Arba'a (ארבעה)	Arba (ארבע)
5	Chamisha (חמישה)	Chamesh (חמש)
6	Shisha (שישה)	Shesh (שש)
7	Shiv'a (שבעה)	Sheva (שבע)
8	Shmonah (שמונה)	Shmoneh (שמונה)
9	Tish'a (תשעה)	Teysha (תשע)
10	Asara (עשרה)	Eser (עשר)

Note: The apostrophe used in the word for Nine and Four often appears as a marker for the letters Aleph and Ayin when they appear in awkward places. Look at the Hebrew to verify the pronunciation.

Numbers 11-20

Number	Masculine Form	Feminine Form
11	Echad Asar (אחד עשר)	Achat Esrei (אחת עשרה)
12	Shneim Asar (שנים עשר)	Shteim Esrei (עשרה שתים)
13	Shlosha Asar (שלושה עשר)	Shalosh Esrei (שלוש עשרה)
14	Arba'a Asar (ארבעה עשר)	Arba Esrei (עשרה ארבע)
15	Chamisha Asar (חמישה עשר)	Chamesh Esrei (עשרה חמש)
16	Shisha Asar (ששה עשר)	Shesh Esrei (עשרה שש)
17	Shiva Asar (שבעה עשר)	Shva Esrei (עשרה שבע)
18	Shmonah Asar (שמונה עשר)	Shmoneh Esrei (עשרה שמונה)

19	Tish'a Asar (תשעה עשר)	Tisha Esrei (עשרה תשע)
20	Esrim (עשרים)	Esrim (עשרים)

*For 21-29 it follows this pattern: Esrim + number 1-10

Ex: 21 --->   Esrim Ve-Echad, 22 --->   Esrim Ve-Shtaim, 23 ---> Esrim Ve-Shalosh, etc.

Numbers 30-100+

30	Shloshim (שלושים)
40	Arba'im (ארבעים)
50	Chamishim (חמשים)
60	Shishim (ששים)
70	Shiv'im (שבעים)
80	Shmonim (שמונים)
90	Tish'im (תשעים)
100	Mey-ah (מאה)
105	Mey-ah Ve-Chamesh (Feminine), Mey-ah Ve-Chamisha (Masculine)
115	Mey-ah Ve-Chamesh Esrei (Feminine), Mey-ah Ve-Chamisha Asar (Masculine)

*For 31-99 it follows this pattern: Ten + number as two separate words

Ex:	33	=	Shloshim Ve Shalosh
	45	=	Arba'im Ve Chamesh
	78	=	Shiv'im Ve Shmoneh

* For 101 to 199, just say Mey-ah + the number
Ex: 190= Mey'ah Ve Tishim (see examples above)

Numbers 200-1000

200	Matayim (מאתיים)
300	Shalosh May'ot (מאות שלוש)
400	Arba May'ot (מאות ארבע)
500	Chamesh May'ot (מאות חמש)
600	Shesh May'ot (מאות שש)
700	Shva May'ot (מאות שבע)
800	Shmonah May'ot (מאות שמונה)
900	Tisha May'ot (מאות תשע)
1000	Elef (אלף)

Colors

Red	Adom/Aduma (ה/אדום)
Orange	Katom/Ketuma (כתום/ה)
Yellow	Tsahov/Tsehuva (ה/צהוב)
Green	Yarok/Yeruka (ה/ירוק)
Blue	Kachol/Kechula (ה/כחול)
Purple	Seggol/Seggula (ה/סגול)
Pink	Varod/Vruda (ה/ורוד)
Black	Shachor/Shechura (ה/שחור)
White	Lavan/Levana (ה/לבן)
Brown	Chum/Chuma (ה/חום)
Gray	Afor/Afura (ה/אפור)

Note: I will generally include both masculine and feminine forms. If you see one Hebrew word, it means the spelling is the same but the vowels are different.

Other useful vocabulary and phrases

Yes	Ken (כֵּן)
No	Lo (לֹא)
But	Aval (אֲבָל)
also/too	Gam (גַם)
And	Ve- (This is a prefix placed before a noun)(ו)
In	Be- (This is a prefix placed before a noun)(ב)
With	Im (עִם)
Or	o (אוֹ)
Now	Achshav (עַכְשָׁיו)
Because	Ki, Mipnei She-, Biglal (usage depends on context) (כִּי, מִפְּנֵי שֶׁ־, בִּגְלַל)
Sorry	Slicha (סְלִיחָה)
Excuse Me	Slicha (סְלִיחָה)
Thank you	Todah (תּוֹדָה)
You're Welcome	BeVakasha (בְּבַקָשָׁה)
Please	BeVakasha (בְּבַקָשָׁה)
Me Too	Gam Ani (גַם אֲנִי)
Very	Me'od (מְאוֹד)
A lot	Harbey (הַרְבֵּה)

That's okay/Okay	Zeh BeSeder/BeSeder (זה בסדר/בסדר)

Chapter 4
Greetings, Introductions, and Other Useful Phrases

?מה נשמע

In this chapter we will go over the very different ways to greet and introduce yourself to others. Below is a list of common greetings in Hebrew.

Common Greetings

Hello	Shalom, Ahlan (This is a borrowing from Arabic that is commonly used in Israel) (שלום, אהלן)
Good Morning	Boker Tov (בוקר טוב)
Good Afternoon	Tsahorayim Tovim (צהרים טובים)
Good evening/Good night	Erev Tov (ערב טוב)
General Greeting	Shalom or Ahlan (שלום, אהלן)

Asking and Answering 'How are you?'

How are you? (informal)	Mah Nishma? or Mah Koreh (מה קורה/מה נשמע)
How are you doing? (informal)	Mah Nishma? or Mah Koreh (מה קורה/מה נשמע)
How are you doing?(formal)	Mah Shlomcha/Shlomech? (מה שלומך)
How are you?	Mah Nishma? or Mah Koreh (מה קורה/מה נשמע)
Well/Very well	B'Seder (בסדר)
Good and you? (informal)	Tov ve-at/a? (ואת טוב/ה)

Good and you? (formal)	Tov ve-at/a? (?ה/ואת טוב)
So-so	Kacha-Kacha (ככה ככה)
What's up? What's new?	Mah Nishma? or Mah Chadash? (חדש מה/נשמע מה)

Saying Goodbye

English	Hebrew
Goodbye	Lehitra'ot (להתראות)
See you later	Lehitra'ot (להתראות)
Bye	Lehitra'ot (להתראות)

Hazara!

Translate the following conversation into English

#1

- Shalom Moshe (משה שלום) ----->

- Ahlan Einat! (עינת אהלן) ----->

- Mah Nishma? (נשמע מה)----->

- HaKol BeSeder.   Ve-at? (ואת .בסדר הכל) ----->

- Mitzuyan, todah. (תודה ,מצוין) ----->

- Lehitra'ot, Einat. (עינת ,להתראות) ----->

-Lehishtameah, Moshe! (משה ,להשתמע) ----->

*Did you notice there were words not listed in the vocabulary above? Were you able to use context clues and fill in the rest of the meaning?   This is a great skill to have because most of the time there will be words you may not understand.

Introductions and Other phrases

What is your name? (informal)	Eych Kor'im Lecha/Lach? (איך קוראים לך)
My name is...	Shmi.... ; Korim Li...... (שמי..../קוראים לי)
Nice to meet you!	Na'im Me'od (נעים מאוד)
It's a pleasure.	Na'im Me'od (נעים מאוד)
Me too.	Gam Ani. (גם אני)
Where are you from?	Me-Efo Atah/At? (מאיפה אתה/את)
I am from the U.S.	Ani Me-Artzot HaBrit (אני מארצות הברית)
How old are you?	Ben Kama Ata/Bat Kama At? (בן כמה אתה/בת כמה את)
I am... years old.	Ani ben/bat....shanim. (אני בן/בת...שנים)
Canada	Canada (קנדה)
England	Angliah (אנגליה)
South Africa	Drom Africa (דרום אפריקה)
Australia	Australia (אוסטרליה)

Cultural Note: **Kissing** — In Israel, kissing on the cheek with a greeting is normal amongst some groups, specifically amongst Sephardic Jews.   It isn't always acceptable amongst the religious, especially between men and women who are not related.

*Below, I will list some useful phrases for when you don't understand, are confused or need clarification, something common when learning a language.

Other Useful Phrases

I don't understand.	Ani Lo Mevin or Lo Hevanti (אני לא מבין/לא הבנתי)
Can you repeat, please.	Od Pa'am, BeVakasha (literally: Again please) (עוד פעם בבקשה)
Speak more slowly, please.	Tidaber yoter le'at bevakasha (תדבר יותר לאט בבקשה)
How do you say ...?	Eych Omrim? (...איך אומרים)
What does this mean?	Mah Zeh/Zot omer/et? (מה זה/זאת אומר/ת)
What is this?	Mah Zeh? (זה מה)
Can you help me?	Ulai Ta'azor li? (אולי תעזור לי)
Do you speak English?	Medaber Anglit? (מדבר אנגלית)
I speak a little Hebrew.	Ani Midaber Kitzat Ivrit (עברית קצת מדבר אני)
I don't know.	Ani Lo Yodeah/Yoda'at (or just Lo Yodeah/Yoda'at) (אני לא יודעת, לא יודע/ת)
Write it down, please.	Tichtov et zeh, bevakasha. (תכתוב את זה, בבקשה)

Hazara!

Translate the following conversation into English

#2

- Tzahorayim tovim! (טובים צהרים) ----->

- Shalom!   Mah Koreh? (קורה מה !שלום)   ----->

- HaKol BeSeder, Todah.   Ve-At? (וְאַתְּ .בְּסֵדֶר הַכֹּל ,תּוֹדָה) ----->

- Kacha-kacha, todah.   (כָּכָה–כָּכָה ,תּוֹדָה) ----->

- Eych Korim Lach? (לָךְ קוֹרְאִים אֵיךְ) ----->

- Korim Li Na'ama.   Mah Shimcha? (שִׁמְךָ מַה .נְעֲמָה לִי קוֹרְאִים) ----->

- Ani D'vir. (אֲנִי דְּבִיר) ----->

- Ben Kama Atah? (בֶּן כַּמָה אַתָּה) ----->

- Ani ben 23.   Ve-at? (וְאַתְּ .23 בֶּן אֲנִי) ----->

- Ani bat 27.   Me-Efo atah? (אַתָּה מֵאֵיפֹה .27 בַּת אֲנִי) ----->

- Ani mi-Germania.   Me-efo at? (אַתְּ מֵאֵיפֹה .מִגֶּרְמַנְיָה אֲנִי) ----->

- Ani me-Tel Aviv. (אָבִיב מִתֵּל אֲנִי) ——>

- Na'im Me-od.   (מְאֹד נָעִים) ——>

- Tov lehakircha! (לְהַכִּירְךָ טוֹב) ——>

Match the Phrases
1. I speak a little Hebrew----------------------------a. Medaber Anglit?
2. Write it down, please. ----------------------------b. Eych Omrim?
3. Do you speak English? ——————————c.Od Pa'am Bevakasha?
4. I don't understand. --------------------------------d. Tidaber yoter le'at bevakasha
5. How do you say…?————   ————e. Tichtov et Zeh bevakasha.
 6. I don't know. -------------------------------------f. Ani Lo Yode'ah.
 7. Speak slowly please. ----------------------------g. Mah Zeh?
  8.   Can you repeat, please? -----------------------h. Ani medaber ketzat Ivrit.
  9.   What is this? ------------------------------------i. Ani Lo Mayvin.
10. What does this mean? -------------------------j. Mah Zeh omer?

Chapter 4 Answers

Translation #1

- Shalom Moshe
- Ahlan Einat!
- Mah Nishma?
- HaKol BeSeder.   Ve-at?
- Mitzuyan, todah.
- Lehitra'ot, Einat.
-Lehishtameah, Einat!

- Hi Moshe!
-    Hi Einat!
- How's it going?
- Very good, thanks. And you?
- Excellent, thanks.
- Bye Einat.
- See ya Moshe!

Translation #2

- Tzahorayim tovim! ----->
- Shalom!   Mah Koreh? ----->
- HaKol BeSeder, Todah.   Ve-At? ----->
- Kacha-kacha, todah.   ----->
- Eych Korim Lach?? ----->
- Korim Li Na'ama.   Mah Shimcha? ----->
- Ani D'vir.   ----->
- Ben Kama At? ----->
- Ani bat 23.   Ve-atah? ----->
- Ani ben 27.   Me-Efo at? ----->
- Ani mi-Germania.   Me-efo atah? ----->
- Ani me-Tel Aviv ----->
- Na'im Me-od. ——>
- Tov lehakircha!——>

- Good afternoon!
- Hi! How are you?

- Good, thanks. And you?
- So so, thank you.
- What's your name?
- My name is Na'ama, And what is your name?
- I'm Dvir.
- How old are you?
- I am 23 years old and you?
- I'm 27 years old. Where are you from?
- I am from Germany. Where are you from?
- I am from Tel Aviv
- Nice to meet you!
- Nice to meet you!

Note: The Hebrew text was included here so you can get a feel for reading Hebrew.   I will do this with conversations only.

Match the Phrases

1. I speak a little Hebrew. -----------c. Ani medaber ketzat Ivrit.
2. Write it down, please. ------------g. Tichtov et zeh bevakasha.
  3. Do you speak English?   -----------h. Medaber Anglit?
  4. I don't understand. ---------------b. Ani lo mayvin.
  5. How do you say…?----------------i. Eych omrim?
6. I don't know. -----------------------d. Ani lo yode'ah
7. Speak slowly please.--------------e. Tidaber yoter le'at bevakasha.
  8.   Can you repeat, please?---------j. Od ma'am bevakasha?
  9.   What is this?---------------------a. Mah zeh?
10. What does this mean? ----------f. Mah zen omer?

Chapter 5
About Time - Telling time, Days of Week, Dates

In this chapter, I will discuss how to talk about time, telling time, days of week, months, etc. Time has a funny place in Israeli culture. While it might be acceptable to be late to a gathering with friends, that is not the case in the business world where punctuality is valued. However, many people are much more relaxed in regards to time. This is partially rooted in the joke term of Jewish Standard Time which is always about 15 minutes late. In Israel it is also highly recommended to bring a book when you go to government offices.

Telling Time

What time is is?	Mah HaSha'ah? (מה השעה)
It's one.	HaSha'ah Echad. (אחד השעה)
It's two.	HaSha'ah Shtaim. (שתיים השעה)
It's four thirty.	HaSha'ah Arba VaChetzi (literally four and a half) (וחצי ארבע השעה)
It's fifteen until eight.	HaSha'ah Reva LeShmoneh (literally a quarter of five) (לשמונה רבע השעה)
a.m. (in the morning)	BaBoker (בבוקר)
p.m. (in the afternoon)	BaTzahorayim (בצהרים)
p.m. (at night)	BaErev (בערב)

* If you want to add minutes to the hour, the format Ve _____ dakot

    Ex: It is 6:05   =   HaSha'ah Shesh VeChamisha Dakot.

Now you try:

1. It is 3:05_____

2. It is 10:45_____

3. It is 8:20_____

*If you want to say that it is 15 til, 10 til, or 5 til an hour, use the following formation:

It is ten til five = HaSha'ah Asara leChamesh.

Now you try:

4. It is fifteen til three_____
5. It is five til seven _____
6. It is ten til nine_____

Days of the Week

What day is today?	Aizeh Yom Hayom? (איזה יום היום)
Today is Thursday	Ha-Yom yom chamishi. (היום יום חמישי)
Today	HaYom (היום)
Yesterday	Etmol (אתמול)
Tomorrow	Machar (מחר)
Monday	Yom Sheni (יום שני)
Tuesday	Yom Shlishi (יום שלישי)
Wednesday	Yom Rivee'ee (יום רביעי)
Thursday	Yom Chamishee (יום חמישי)
Friday	Yom Sheeshee (Erev Shabbat) (יום ששי/ערב שבת)
Saturday	Shabbat (שבת)

Sunday	Yom Rishon (יום ראשון)

* When you say *On Monday I'm going to the doctor ---> BeYom Sheni Ani holech le-rofeh* you use the prefix be- that means literally *in*.

Talking about the Date

What is the date today?	Mah HaTa'arich HaYom? (מה התאריך היום?)
Today is February 15th	Hayom Chamesh Esrei LeFebruar; Hayom Chamesh Esrei le Sheni (לשני עשרה חמש היום/בפברואר עשרה חמש היום)
January	Yanuar (ינואר)
February	Februar (פברואר)
March	Mertz (מרץ)
April	April (אפריל)
May	may (מאי)
June	yuni (יוני)
July	yuli (יולי)
August	August (אוגוסט)
September	September (ספטמבר)
October	October (אוקטובר)
November	November (נובמבר)
December	Detzember (דצמבר)

*The Jewish calendar has a different set of months with a different new year known as Rosh Hashanah.   This calendar is generally not referenced outside of religious communities   When it is, it is only in reference to Jewish

holidays.   Do note that in Israel the Jewish calendar is used in school until 5th grade.

Hazara!

Choose the correct answer

7. Mah HaSha'ah?

a. HaSha'ah Shalosh Baboker ----------------------b. Shalosh BeTzahorayim

c. Shmoneh BaBoker ---------------------- d. HaSha'ah Shmoneh BaBoker

8. HaYom yom Shishi.

a. Today is Wednesday ---------------------- b. Today is Friday

c. Today is Sunday   ---------------------- d. Today is Tuesday.

9. Today is March 27th

a. HaTa'arich Hayom 27 Be-Martz ---------------------- b. 27 LaShlishi

c. HaYom 27 LaMartz ---------------------- d. Ha Ta'arich Hayom hu 27 LeMartz

10. It is ten til seven

a. Achshav HaSha'ah Sheva   VeChamishim.——————————— b. Reva LeSheva

c. Achshav HaSha'ah asara leSheva ---------------------- d. Hasha'ah Sheva VeChetzi.

11. It is 3:15?

a. Higanu LeShalosh VaReva?---------------------- b. HaSha'ah Shalosh VeReva?

c. HaSha'ah Shalosh va-asara? ----------------------d. HaSha'ah Shalosh VeChamesh Esrei?

Chapter 5 Answers

1. It is 3:05 ----> HaSha'ah Shalosh VeChamisha Dakot or HaSha'ah Shalosh VeChamisha.

2. It is 10:45 ----> HaSha'ah Reva Le-Echad Esrei or HaSha'ah Asarah Arba'im Ve-Chamesh.

3. It is 8:20 ----> HaSha'ah Shmoneh Ve-Esrim.

4. It is fifteen til three. ----> HaSha'ah Reva Le-Shalosh.

5. It is five til seven. ----> HaSha'ah Chamisha LeSheva.

6. It is ten til nine. ----> HaSha'ah Asara Le-Teysha.

Choose the correct answer

7. Mah HaSha'ah?

a. HaSha'ah Shalosh Baboker.

8. HaYom yom Shishi.

b. Today is Friday.

9. Today is March 27th

a. HaTa'arich Hayom 27 Be-Martz.

10. It is ten til seven

c. Achshav HaSha'ah asara leSheva

11. It is 3:15?

b. HaSha'ah Shalosh VeReva?

Chapter 6
How Do You Like This Weather?

?היום התחזית מה

This chapter will discuss how to talk about the weather, something people will comment on when it is extremely hot outside or very rainy.   This can be useful when in Israel in the summer when it is hot most of the time or during the winter when the rain can come out of nowhere. It is also handy because Israel sometimes has sandstorms pass through.   Below are some useful phrases and vocabulary to use when talking about the weather.

Weather Expressions

What's the weather like today?	Mah HaMezeg Ha-Avir Hayom? Mah HaTechazit hayom? (what's the forecast for today?) (היום התחזית מה/היום האויר המזג מה)
Cold	Kar (קר)
Hot	Cham (חם)
Sunny	Bahir (literally, clear) (בהיר)
Windy	So'er (literally stormy) (סוער)
The weather is nice	Mezeg Ha'Avir Naim. (נעים האויר מזג)
The weather is bad	Mezeg Ha'avir Lo Tov. (טוב לא האויר מזג)
It's cool.	Karir (קריר)
It's raining.	Gashum (גשום)
Is it going to rain today?	Yored Geshem HaYom? (היום גשם יורד)
Yes, it's going to rain, No, it's not going to rain	Ken, Yered Geshem\Lo Yered Geshem (גשם ירד לא ,גשם ירד כן)
It's snowing	Shalug (שלוג)

Really?	Be'Emet? (באמת)
Heat wave (not sand storm)	Chamsin (חמסין)
Heat wave (with a sandstorm)	Sharav (שרב)

* If you want to say: It is very hot, cold, etc. you use Me'od. Me'od means *very*.

Ex: It is very hot ——> Cham Me'od

It is very cold ----> Kar Me'od

A more colloquial form of this is *Eyzeh kor/chom*, that literally means "What cold/heat!"
If you want to say "I'm cold/hot" you say "Kar/Cham li" that literally means *it is cold/hot to me*.

Hazara!

Choose the correct answer

1. Ma HaMezeg Ha'Avir Hayom?

a. Yihyeh kar me'od. -----------------b. Yihyeh bahir.

c. Yihyeh cham me'od. ----------------- d. Yered geshem hayom.

2. It is very sunny today.

a. Bahir me'od hayom ----------------- b. Yesh Shemesh Hayom.

c. Cham me'od hayom. ----------------- d. Lo bahir hayom.

3. Yered geshem hayom?

a. Lo yered geshem Hayom. ----------------- b. Ken veyihyeh gam so'er.

c. Lo, yihyeh bahir. ----------------- d. Ken yered geshem.

Translate to Hebrew

- Hi friend, how are you?

- Good! How is the weather today?

- It's nice! It's not going to rain.

- But, it is very windy.

- Yes, but very sunny too.

- See you tomorrow!

- Goodbye!

Chapter 6 Answers

Choose the correct answer

1. Ma HaMezeg Ha'Avir Hayom?

a. Yihyeh kar me'od.

2. It is very sunny today.

a. Bahir me'od hayom

3. Yered geshem hayom?

d. Ken yered geshem.

Translation

- Hi friend, how are you?
- Good! How is the weather today?
- It's nice! It's not going to rain.
- But, it is very windy.
- Yes, but very sunny too.
- See you tomorrow!
- Goodbye!

- Ahlan chaver, mah nishmah?
- Tov! Eych mezeg ha'avir hayom?
- Na'im! Lo yered geshem.
- Ken, aval so'er.
- Ken, aval bahir gam.
- Lehishtame'ah!
- Lehitraot!

SECTION 2
IN THE CITY AND TRAVELING

Chapter 7
Directions (Where Is The...?)

?הבנק איפה

In this chapter we will cover some really useful vocabulary that you will need when in a new country with no idea where anything is. These days with google maps and GPS stopping to ask for directions is less common. In Israel, you'll have easy access to internet.   However, it's easier to ask for directions because it's usually easier to use landmarks than a map to find where you are.   Streets are notorious for changing names in the middle or having a strange numbering order: I lived on a street in Israel where the numbers began at 21, dropped to 20 and then started over from 1 to 18!   So get ready to have to actually talk to people face to face and maybe get lost.   My only advice is to never listen to anyone who says "Yashar Yashar Vesmolah", because they never know what they are talking about!   Here are the most useful phrases and vocabulary for getting around in Hebrew.

Phrases to talk about Directions

Where is it?	Efo....? (איפה...)
Excuse me, where is the…	Slicha, efo ha…? (סליחה, איפה ה...)
It's next to the…	Le-Yad…/Tzmud Le (ליד, צמוד ל)
It's in front of the…	Lifnei… (לפני)
Keep straight	Yashar (ישר)
Turn right	Yemina (ימינה)
Turn left	Smolah (שמאלה)
It's on the right/left	Hu al tzad yamin/smol (הוא על צד ימין/שמאל)
Far from	Rachok me.. (רחוק מ)
Near to	Karov le…. (קרוב ל)
Above	Me-Al (מעל)

Below	MeTachat (מתחת)
Behind	Acharei (אחרי)

Places

The bank	HaBank (הבנק)
The restaurant	HaMis'ada (המסעדה)
The post office	HaDo'ar (ה)
The supermarket	HaSuper, HaMakolet (המכולת, הסופר)
The pharmacy	HaMerkachat (המרקחת)
The bakery	HaMa'afia (המאפיה)
Bus/Train station	Tachanat Otobus/Rakevet (רכבת/אוטובוס תחנת)
Store	Chanut (חנות)
Synagogue	Bet Knesset (כנסת בית)

*Did you notice which words are masculine and feminine?

Other Phrases

I am lost.	Ani avud/a.(אני אבוד/ה)
How do I get to ...?	Eych Ani magia le... (איך אני מגיע ל)
Cross the street.	Ta'avor HaKvish (הכביש תעבור)
Where am I now?	Efo ahi achshav? (איפה אני עכשיו)
the corner	Ha-Pina (הפינה)
street	Rechov (רחוב)
here	Po (פה)

there	Sham (שם)

Time Expressions

Before	Lifnei (לפני)
Now	Achshav (עכשיו)
After	Acharei (אחרי)
Later	Me-Uchar Me... (מ מאוחר)

Hazara!

Choose the correct answer

1. The bank is next to the post office.

a. HaBank acharei hadoar.----- b. Habank Al Yad HaDoar.

c. HaBank al gabei hadoar.-----   d. HaBank tzamud ladoar.

2. Turn right at the bakery.

a. Yemina liyad HaMa'afia.——   b. Tifneh Smola liyah haMa'afia.

c. Tifneh Yemina liyad haMa'afia.----- d. Yemina etzel acharei haramzor haba.

3. The store is close to the synagogue.

a. HaMakolet rachok MeHaBeit HaKnesset.----- b. HaMakolet al yad HaBeit HaKnesset.

c. HaMakolet MeAchorei HaBeit HaKnesset.----- d. HaMakolet karov laBeit HaKnesset.

Translate to English

- Slicha, efo haTachanat Rakevet laRehovot? (סליחה, איפה התחנת הרכבת לרחובות)

- Tamshich Yashar etzel a HaBank Vetifneh smolah BeRehov Jabotinski.
(תמשיך ישר אצל הבנק ותפנה שמאלה בחרוב ג׳בוטינסקי)

- BeSeder (בסדר)

- VeAz Tamshich Yashar, Tifneh Yeminah al Al Parashat Derachim VeHu al hayamin.
(ואז תמשיך ישר, תפנה ימינה על על פרשת דרכים והוא על הימין)

- Beseder.   Hi Rechoka MiPo? (בסדר. היא רחוקה מפה)

- Kitzat, ani choshev shetikach otobus mispar 45 lesham.
(קצת, אני חושב שתיקה אוטובוס מספר 45 לשם)

- Todah raba! (תודה רבה)

- HaLo Davar. (הלא דבר)

Chapter 7 Answers

Choose the correct answer

1. The bank is next to the post office.
b. Habank Al Yad HaDoar.

2. Turn right at the bakery.
c. Tifneh Yamina liyad haMa'afia.

3. The store is close to the church.
d. HaMakolet karov laBeit HaKnesset.

Translation

- Slicha, efo haTachanat Rakevet laRehovot?
- Tamshich Yashar etzel a HaBank Vetifneh smolah BeRehov Jabotinski.
- BeSeder
- VeAz Tamshich Yashar, Tifeh Yeminah al Al Parashat Derachim VeHu al hayamin.
- Beseder.   Hu Rachok MiPo?
- Kitzat, ani choshev shetikach otobus mispar 45 lesham. HaNahag yagid lecha efo laredet.
- Todah raba!
- HaLo Davar.

- Excuse me, where is the train station to Rehovot?
- Keep straight past the bank and turn left on Jabotinski St.
- Ok.
- Then go straight, turn right on Al Parashat Derachim and it's on the right.
- Okay.   Is that far from here?
- A bit, take the 45 bus there. The driver will tell you where to get off.
- Thank you very much!
- No problem.

Chapter 8
Shopping

?עולה זה כמה

Now, let's move onto that thing we do in other countries - shopping! Whether it be shopping for lame-o souvenirs for your friends and family or shopping for some clothes for yourself, we've got the basics to help you bargain and find what you are looking for. Remember that bargaining can be a big part of shopping in the markets in Hebrew.   If you don't do it, you definitely will get taken advantage of by some lucky shopkeepers who see the 'American' coming from a mile away.   Just keep in mind the somewhat strange culture when standing in line to checkout.   It's totally okay to ask someone to save your spot, disappear for 20 minutes and then come back when it's time to pay for what you bought.   So, let's see if we can find you a great deal!

Shopping phrases

How can I help you?	Eych ani yachol la'azor lecha/lach? (איך אני יכול לעזור לך)
How much does it cost?	Kama zen oleh? or kama zeh? (עולה זה כמה)
How much is it?	Kama Zeh? (זה כמה)
Which one do you want?	Ezeh Mehem At/ah Rotzeh/ah? (איזה מהם את/ה רוצה)
I would like that one.	Ani Rotzeh Et Zeh/Zot. (זאת/זה את רוצה אני)
It's too expensive	Yakar Midai (מדי יקר)
Do you have...?	Ha'im Yesh lecha.... or Yesh lecha... (לך יש/לך יש האם)
Do you have bigger/smaller?	Yesh lecha/lach yoter gadol/katan? (קטן/גדול יותר לך יש)
Do you accept credit cards?	Atem lokchim kartisei ashrai? (אשראי כרטיסי לוקחים אתם)

We only accept cash.	Anachnu rak lokchim mezuman. (מזומן לוקחים רק אנחנו)
Can I try it on?	Efshar limdod? (אפשר למדוד)
I'm just looking.	Ani Rak Mistakel. (מסתכל רק אני)
Of course!	BeVa'adaut or BeHechlet (בהחלט/בודאות)

Shopping Vocabulary

souvenirs	Mazkerot (מזכרות)
clothes	Begadim (בגדים)
shirt	Chultzah (חלצה)
pants	Mechnasayim (מכנסיים)
shorts	Mechnasayim Ketzarot (קצרות מכנסיים)
a dress	Simla (שמלה)
a jacket	Me'il (מעיל)
shoes	Na'alayim (נעליים)
cap	Kovah (כובע)
keychain	Machzik maftechot (מפתחות מחזיק)

Below are the demonstrative adjectives in Hebrew. They are useful when shopping.

Demonstrative Adjectives (This, That, These, Those)

*Note: These also change according to gender and number

This and That

English	Masculine	Feminine	Gender Neutral (When you don't know}
This	Zeh (זה)	Zot (זאת)	Zeh (זה)
That	Hahu (ההוא)	Hahi (ההיא)	Hahu (ההוא)

These and Those

English	Masculine	Feminine
These	Eleh (אלֹה)	Eleh (אלֹה)
Those	Hahem (ההם)	Hahen (ההן)

Remember to keep gender in mind.

Ex: HaYeled Hahu = That child

HaMakolet HaZot = This store

HaChatul Hazeh   = This cat

HaSefarim HaEleh (or Elu) = These books

Note: The default for referring to anything in Hebrew is the masculine form unless you know for sure the group to be referred to in the feminine form. This goes as so far that if you have a group of women and one man, the group is referred to in the masculine form.   The same is true if you have a group of objects to be referred to in the feminine and one that is not.   All of the languages in Hebrew's family do this.   Other languages do this as well. However, keep in mind that this is not always the case.   And ironically enough, the word for *group* in Hebrew is the feminine form word *Kevutzah* (קבוצה) whose plural is *Kevutzot* (קבוצות).

Hazara!

Choose the correct answer

1. HaBanim

a. HaHu.-----b. HaZot

c. HaHem.-----d. HaHena.

2. I would like these shoes.

a. Ani tzarich hamichnasayim ha'eleh. .----- b. Ani rotzeh haNa'alayim HaEleh.

c. Ani lo me'unyan bana'alayim haeleh. .----- d. Ani lo rotzeh ha na'alayim haeleh.

3. Would you like this skirt?

a. At rotzah HaChatza'it Hazot?----- b. HaIm at rotzah ha-michnasayim ha-eleh?

c. At rotzah HaGarbayim HaEleh? .----- d. HaIm At Rotzah HaChatza'it Hazot?

Translate to English

- Boker tov.   Eych Ani yachol la'azor lecha? (בוקר טוב. איך אני יכול לעזור לך)

- Rak mistakel, todah. (רק מסתכל, תודה)

- BeSeder. (בסדר)

- Kama HaChultzah Hazot?   (כמה החלצה הזאת)

- Shalosh Me'ot VeShiv'im Shekel.   (שלוש מאות ושבעים שקל)

- At tzocheket alai!   Yoter midai yakar!   Kama hamichasayim haeleh? (את צוחקת עלי! יותר מדי יקר! כמה המכנסים האלה)

- Me'ah vetish'im shekel. (מאה ותשעים שקל)

- Efshar limdod? (אפסר למדוד)

- BeHechlet! (בהחלט)

- Lokchim Ashrai? (לוקחים אשראי)

- Ken aval ma'adif mezuman. (כן אול מעדיף מזומן)

-    Beseder, Todah Rabah. (בסדר, תודה רבה)

Chapter 8 Answers

Choose the correct answer

1. HaBanim
c. HaHem.

2. I would like these shoes.
b. Ani rotzeh haNa'alayim HaEleh.

3. Would you like this jacket?
d. HaIm At Rotzah HaChatza'it Hazot?

Translation
- Boker tov.   Eych Ani yachol la'azor lecha?
- Rak mistakel, todah.
- BeSeder.
- Kama HaChultzah Hazot?
- Shalosh Me'ot VeShiv'im Shekel.
- At tzocheket alai!   Yoter midai yakar!   Kama hamichasayim haeleh?
- Me'ah vetish'im shekel.
- Efshar limdod?
- BeHechlet!
- Lokchim Ashrai?
- Ken aval ma'adif mezuman.
-    Beseder, Todah Rabah.

- Good morning, how can I help you?
- I'm just looking, thanks.
- Your welcome.
- How much does this shirt cost?
- 370 shekels.
- You're kidding! That's way too expensive And these pants?
- 190 shekels.
- Can I try them on?
- Of course!
- Do you accept credit cards?
- Yes, but prefer cash.
    Okay, thank you very much.

* At tzocheket alai is an expression that means "Are you joking?!" but literally means "You're laughing at me!".   I've never heard it used other than in the context of being surprised and specifically when shopping.

Chapter 9
Going out to eat

אני רוצה להזמין שווארמה בלאפה!

Now we'll move on to food - everyone's favorite thing to do when visiting a new country.   I suggest not expecting the same type of service that you get back home.   Also, tips are never included in the bill except for in fancy restaurants. Let's get ready to eat! BeTe'avon!

Restaurant phrases

What can I bring you?	Mah efshar lehavi lecha/lach? (מה אפשר להביא לך)
I would like to eat...	Ani rotzeh le-echol (אני רוצה לאכול)
I would like to drink...	Ani rotzeh LiShtot (אני רוצה לשתות)
Menu, please	HaTafrit Bevakasha. (התפריט בבקשה)
What do you recommend?	Mah at/atah mamlitz? (מה אתה ממליץ)
Can you bring me?	Efshar lehavi li.... (אפשר להביא)
Excuse me, sir	Slicha adoni (סליחה אדוני)
Excuse me, ma'am	Slicha geveret (סליחה גברת)
Drink	Lishtot (לשתות)
A glass	Kos (כוס)
Soft Drink	Mei Soda (מי סודה)

Juice	Mitz (מיץ)
A glass of water	Kos mayim (כוס מים)
A beer	birah (בירה)
A glass of wine	Kos Yayin (כוס יין)
Dessert	Kinu'ach (קינוח)
Tip	Tip, Sherut (טיפ, שירות)
check, please	HaCheshbon BeVakasha (בבקשה החשבון)

Food Vocabulary

What does this dish have?	Mah yesh banana hazot? (מה יש במנה הזאת)
Does this dish have…?	Halm Yesh _____ bamanah hazot? (האם יש...במנה הזאת)
Meat	Basar (בשר)
Fish	Dag, Dagim (דג)
Chicken	Tarnegol, Tarnegolim (תרנגול)
Ham	Chazir (חזיר)
Egg	Beitzah, Beiztim (ביצה)
Pasta	Pasta, Pastot (פסטה)
Salad	Salat, Salatim (סלט)
Bread	Lechem (לחם)
Cheese	Gvinah, Gvinot (גבינה)
Vegetables	Yerakot (ירקות)
Breakfast	Aruchat Boker (ארוחת בוקר)

Lunch	Aruchat Tzahorayim (ארוחת צהריים)
Dinner	Aruchat Erev (ארוחת ערב)
There is/there are	Yesh/Yeshno (יש/ישנו)

Note: Some of these words have a plural form: The masculine plural adds -im as a suffix and the feminine adds -ot.

Ex: **Dag** becomes **Dagim**; **Arucha** (meal) becomes **Aruchot**

Hazara!

Choose the correct answer

1. This dish has fish, vegetables, and bread.

a. Yesh dagim, peirot ve lechem.
b. Yesh dagim, yerakot velechem.
c. Yesh gvinah, dagim ve yerakot.
d. Yesh yerakot, peirot vebasar.

2. Can you bring me a beer please?
a. Efshar tavi li bira bevakasha?
  b. Tavi li mayim bevakasha.
c. Ulai tavi li kos bira?
d. Ani rotzeh lishtot birah.   Tavi li, Bevakasha.

3. Excuse me ma'am, the check please.
a. Slicha adoni, ani rotzeh od bira.
b. Slicha geveret, efshar od mayim?
c. Slicha chaver, efshar lihavi hacheque?
d. Slicha geveret, hacheshbon bevakasha.

4. LeAruchat erev yesh tarnegol, lechem veyerakot.
a. For breakfast there are eggs, chicken and vegetables.
b. For dinner there is chicken, bread and vegetables.
c. For breakfast there is bread, vegetables and beer.
d. For dinner there are vegetables, lasagna and soda water.

5. Acharei aruchat boker ani rotzeh kos kafe.
a. Before lunch, I would like dessert.
b. After dinner, I would like a beer.
c. After breakfast, I'd like a cup of coffee.
d. After lunch, I would like a cookie.

Translate to English

- Erev tov.   Mah efshar lehavi lecha? (ערב טוב. מה אפשר להביא לך)

- Mah at mamlitzah? (מה את ממליצה)

- Ani mamlitz ha special shel hayom, yesh bo marak basar teimani, lechem veyerakot.
(אני ממליץ הספשל של היום, יש בו מרק בשר תימני, לחם וירקות)

- Beseder az ani azmin oto. (בסדר אז אני אזמין אתו)

- Mashehu lishtot? (משהו לשתות)

- Rak mayim bevakasha. (רק מים בבקשה)

- Beseder gamur. (בסדר גמור)

- Todah raba. (תודה רבה)

Chapter 9 Answers

Choose the correct answer

1. This dish has fish, vegetables, and bread.
b. Yesh dagim, yerakot velechem.

2. Can you bring me a beer please?
a. Efshar tavi li bira bevakasha?

3. Excuse me ma'am, the check please.
d. Slicha geveret, hacheshbon bevakasha.

4. LeAruchat erev yesh tarnegol, lechem veyerakot.

b. For dinner there is chicken, bread and vegetables.

5. Acharei aruchat boker ani rotzeh kos kafe.

c. After breakfast, I'd like a cup of coffee.

Translate to English

- Erev tov.   Mah efshar lehavi lecha?
- Mah at mamlitzah?
- Ani mamlitz ha special shel hayom, yesh bo marak bazar teimani, lechem veyerakot.
- Beser az ani azmin oto.
- Mashehu lishtot?
- Rak mayim bevakasha.
- Beseder gamur.
- Todah raba.

- Good evening. What can I bring you?
- What do you recommend?
- I recommend today's special, it consists of Yemenite meat soup, bread and vegeable.
- Okay, I'll order that.
- And to drink?
- Just water please.
- Okay.
- Thank you.

Chapter 10
Going to the Doctor

איפה כואב לך?

Let's talk something you really don't want to do when you're not home: Going to the doctor.   This can be really difficult if you don't speak the language. Even though Israelis have really good English and by law all clinics and offices must have an English speaker, its better to be able to explain yourself in Hebrew.   While I have never had to go to the hospital for anything food related, I've definitely had to go to the doctor to get medication.   Below are some basic and useful phrases to use when you are sick, going to the doctor or hospital.

Phrases to use at the Doctor

What's wrong?	Mah kara? (literally what happened? (מה קרה)
I am sick.	Ani Choleh/ah (חולה אני)
I have a cold.	Ani metzunan/metzunenet (אני מצונן/ת)
I have a headache.	Yesh li Ke'ev Rosh (ראש כאב לי יש)
Sore throat	ke'ev garon (כאב גרון)
You should rest.	Atah/At tzarich/tzricha Lanuach (לנוח ה/צריך ה/את)
Injection	Hazraka (הזרקה)
Cough	Mishta'el (משתעל)
Fever	Chom (חום)
Medicine	Trupah (תרופה)
Prescription	Rashum (רשום)
Here is …	Hiney… (הנה)

Do you have health insurance?	Yesh lecha/lach bituach refu'i? (יש לך ביטוח רפואי)

More Doctor Visit Vocabulary

Where does it hurt?	Efo Ko'ev Lecha/Lach? (איפה כואב לך)
It hurts here.	Ko'ev Po. (פה כואב)
My ... hurts.	Ko'ev li........ (...כואב לי ה)
Head	Rosh (ראש)
Arm	Yad (יד)
Leg	Regel (רגל)
Stomach	Beten (בטן)
Hand	Yad (יד)
Foot	Regel (רגל)
Eyes	Eynayim (עיניים)
Nose	Af (אף)
Mouth	Peh (פה)
Ear/Inner ear	Ozen (אוזן)
Chest	Chazeh (חזה)
I have diarrhea	Yesh li Shilshul (יש לי שילשול)
I have been vomiting	Ani meki (אני מקיא)

*When you want to talk about something that hurts

My leg hurts=   Ko'ev Li haregel.

His/her head hurts= Rosho/a/Rosh shelo/shela ko'ev.

Does your hand hurt = Ko'ev lecha hayad? or Hayad ko'ev lecha?

It is backwards and literally means *hurting me the leg is, etc.* Yes, this word order sounds like how Yoda talks, but this is pretty standard in Hebrew. It also appears in other Semitic languages as well, such as in Arabic. In Hebrew, it hearkens to Biblical Hebrew forms, some of which appear in the modern language.

Note: There is more than one way to express ownership in Hebrew. You can attach a single syllable to the end of a word or use conjugations with the word *Shel* that means *Belongs to.* Thus, for the phrase *his arm*, you can say *Yad Shelo* or *Yado* and it means the some thing. If you want to say my home, you say *Beyti*, where *Beyt* (*Bayit*) means home and *-i* means mine.

Hazara!

Fill in the blanks.

1. His arm hurts.

_____ shelo _____.

2. My foot hurts.

_____ li _____.

3. Does your head hurt?

¿ Halm_____ lecha_____?

4. Her chest hurts.

_____ ko'ev.

5. Where does it hurt?

_____ ko'ev lecha?

Match the Vocabulary

1. arm -----------------------a. Yad
  2. chest----------------------b. Regel
3. foot -----------------------c. Chazeh
4. hand----------------------d. Ozen
5. ear------------------------e. Kaf Regel
6. eyes----------------------f. Eynayim
7. leg------------------------g. Peh
8. mouth--------------------h. Kaf Yad
9. stomach-----------------i. Rosh
10. head-------------------j. Beten

Translate to English

- Shalom, mah haba'aya hayom? (שלום מאה הבעיה היום?)

- Ani metznunan veyesh li ke'ev rosh. (אני מצונן ויש לי כאב ראש)

  HaIm atah mishta'el or yesh lecha ke'ev garon? (האם אתה משתעל או יש לך כאב גרון)

  Ken, yesh gam zen ve gam zeh. (כן, יש גם זה וגם זה)

  Eyn lecha chom.   Hinei rashum. (אין לך חום. הנה רשום)

  Todah. (תודה)

  Yesh lecha bituach refu'i? (יש לך ביטוח רפואי?)

  Ken. (כן)

  Tov.   Atah chayav lanuach. (טוב. אתה חייב לנוח)

  Beseder, todah raba. (בסדר, תודה רבה)

- Refuah Sheleima. (רפואה שלמה)

Chapter 10 Answers

Fill in the blanks.

1. His arm hurts.
<u>Yad</u> shelo <u>Ko'ev</u>.

2. My foot hurts.
<u>Ko'ev</u> li <u>HaRegel</u>.

3. Does your head hurt?
¿ HaIm   <u>Rosh</u> Shelcha <u>Ko'ev</u>?

4. Her chest hurts.
<u>Chazeha</u> ko'ev.

5. Where does it hurt?
Efo ko'ev lecha?

Match the Vocabulary

1. arm   ----- a. Yad
2. chest-----   c. Chazeh
3. Foot-----   e. Kaf Regel
4. hand ----- h. Kaf Yad
5. ear--------d. Ozen
  6. eyes----- f. Eynayim
  7. leg-------b. Regel
  8. mouth------ g. Peh
  9. stomach----- j. Beten
  10. head----- i. Rosh

Translate to English

- Shalom, mah haba'aya hayom?
- Ani metznunan veyesh li ke'ev rosh.
    HaIm atah mishta'el or yeah lecha ke'ev garon?
    Ken, yesh gam zen ve gam zeh.
    Ain lecha chom.   Hinei rashum.
    Todah.

Yesh lecha bituach refu'i?

Ken.

Tov.   Atah chayav lanuach.

Beseder, todah raba.

- Refuah Sheleima.

- Good afternoon, what's wrong today?
- I have a cold and headache.
- Are you coughing or do you have a sore throat?
- Yes I have both.
- You don't have a fever.   Here is a prescription.
- Thank you.
- Do you have health insurance?
- Yes, I do.
- Okay. You should rest a bit.
- Okay thank you.
- Feel better.

Chapter 11
Going to the Bank

..כסף להפקיד צריך אני

In this chapter we will discuss something that you will need to know so you don't make mistakes with money.   When traveling you may use a credit card, travelers cheques or an ATM card.   You may even open your own bank account. You will need to goto the bank at least once while in Israel.   A word of warning: Israeli banks are notorious for loving paperwork.   Even the most simple of transactions will produce 2-3 pieces of paper.   Opening a bank account will produce a mountain of paper.   You can use it as compost when you get back to your country of origin after you pull out the most important papers.   Here are the most important phrases for dealing with money in Israel.

Banking Phrases

I need to withdraw money	Ani Tzarich/a LiMshoch Kesef (כסף למשוך ה/צריך אני)
deposit money	LeHafkid kesef (כסף להפקיד)
exchange money	LeHamir Kesef (כסף להמיר)
How much is the dollar worth	Kama shaveh hadollar? (הדולר שוה כמה)
I want to open an account?	Ani rotzeh lifto'ach cheshbon. (חשבון לפתוח רוצה אני)
I want to transfer money.	Ani rotzeh la'avor kesef (כסף לעבור רוצה אנ)
Cash	Mezuman (מזומן)
Currency	Matbe'ah (מטבע)

Milon - BaBank

Credit Card	Kartis Ashrai (כרתיס אשראי)
Traveler's cheques	Shekim Nos'im (נוסעים צ׳יקים/שקים)
Account	Cheshbon (חשבון)
Cashier	Kupah (קופה)
ATM	Kaspomat (כספומט)
Loan	Halva'ah (הלוואה)
Identification (ID)	Teudat Zehut (זהות תעודת)
Amount	Schum (סכום)

Hazara!

Match the Vocabulary

1. Kartis ashrai ----------------------------------a. loan
2. Kaspomat——————————————-b. credit card
3. Mezuman——————————————c. amount
4. Schum ——————————————d. cashier
5. LeHamir———————-——————————e. currency
6. Kupah——————————————–f. ATM
7. Chesbon——————————————g. cash
8. Matbe'ah——————————————h. to exchange
9. Shekim Nos'im---------------------------- i. traveler's cheques
10. Halva'ah--------------------------------j. account

Translate to English

- Shalom, eych ani yachol la'azor lach? (שלום, איך אני יכול לעזור לך?)

- Ahlan, ani tazrich lehamir kesef. (אהלן אני צריך להמיר כסף)

- Beseder. (בסדר)

- Kama shaveh hadollar?   (כמה שווה הדולר)

- Hadollar shaveh shalosh vachetzi (3.5) shkalim. (הדולר שווה 3.5 שקלים)

- Beseder, Ani rotzeh lehamir me'ah dollar. (בסדר, אני רוצה להמיר מאה דולר)

- Yihiyeh Shalosh me'ot VeChamishim Shkelim. (יהיה שלוש מאות וחמישים שקלים)

- Todah Rabah. (תודה רבה)

- Bevakasha, ahlah yom. (בבקשה, אחלה יום)

Chapter 11 Answers

Match the Vocabulary

1. Kartis ashrai ----------------------------------b. credit card
2. Kaspomat————————————-f. ATM
3. Mezuman————————————g. cash
4. Schum ————————————c. amount
5. LeHamir————-—————————h. to exchange
6. Kupah———————————--d. cashier
7. Chesbon————————————j. account
8.   Matbe'ah————————————e. currency
9. Shekim Nos'im------------------------- i. traveler's cheques
10. Halva'ah————————————a. loan

Translation

- Shalom, each ahi yachol la'azor lach?
- Ahlan, ahi tazrich lehamir kesef.
- Beseder.
- Kama shaveh hadollar?
- Hadollar shaveh shalosh vachetzi (3.5) shkalim.
- Beseder, Ani rotzeh lehamir me'ah dollar.
- Yihiyeh Shalosh VeChamishim Shkelim.
- Todah Rabah.
- Bevakasha, ahlah yom.

- Hello, how can I help you?
- Hi, I need to exchange money.
- Okay.
- How much is the dollar worth?
- The dollar is worth 3.5 Shekels.
- Okay, I want to exchange 100 dollars.
- That will be 350 shekels.
-Thank you.
- You're welcome, have a great day.

Note: The word *Ahlah* is from Arabic and means great.   *Ahlah Yom* means "have a great day".   A lot of slang terms used in Israel come from Arabic.

Chapter 12
Transportation

?טס אתה לאן

Part 1: At the airport

This chapter will be divided into two sections: *At the Airport* and *Traveling by taxi, bus or train.* The first section is about how to handle first arriving in Israel. Most airport employees speak good English, but some will prefer to speak Hebrew. It will be faster getting through customs and passport control if you can speak a bit of Hebrew. You certainly will be much better off when you get through and are ready to go to wherever your destination is. Tisah Ne'ima!

At the Airport

Airport	Sdei Te'ufa/Namal Te'ufa (שדה תעופה/נמל תעופה)
Airplane	Matos/Aviron (מטוס/אבירון)
Airline	Chevrat Te'ufah (הברת תעופה)
Suitcase	Mizvada/Mizvadot (מזודה, מזודות)
Passport	Darkon (דרכון)
Flight	Tisa (טיסה)
Customs	Meches (מכס)
Ticket	Kartis Tisa (כרטיס טיסה)
Baggage Claim Area	Azor Isuf Mizvadot (אזור איסוף מזודות)
Gate	Sha'ar (שער)
Terminal	Terminal (טרמינל)
Destination	Ya'ad (יעד)
Have a good trip!	Tisa Ne'ima! (טיסה נעימה)

Useful Phrases at the Airport

When does the flight leave?	Matai Yotzeh HaTisa? (הטיסה יוצא מתי)
When does the flight arrive?	Matai Yagi'a HaTisa? (הטיסה יגיע מתי)
I have two suitcases.	Yesh li Shtei Mizvadot (מזודות שתי לי יש)
Where is terminal B?	Efo terminal b? (בי טרמינל איפה)
I'm looking for gate 17.	Ani mechapes sha'ar 17 (17 שער מחפס אני)
Where is the baggage claim?	Efo Isuf Mizvadot? (מזודות איסוף איפע)
My suitcases are lost.	Mizvadot Sheli avudot. (אבודות שלי מזודות)

Hazara!

Fill in the blank with the word from the word bank

Isuf Mizvadot ----- Yotzeh
Terminal Bet ----Yagia
BaMatos----- Sde Te'ufa

1. Ani Michapeset _____.

2. Matai _____ HaTisa?

3. _____ Nimtza BeTzad Hasheni shel _____.

4. Tasti LeNew York _____ Shel Delta.

5. HaTisa yihyeh me'uchar ve _____ be-shtaim baboker.

Match the Vocabulary

6. Ya'ad --------------------a. Airplane

7. Tisa Ne'ima---------------------b. Customs

8. Matos----------------------c. Have a good trip

9. Meches ----------------------d. Ticket

10. Kartis Tisa-------------------e. Destination

Translate to English

- Shalom, Eych ani yachol la'azor? (לעזור יכול אני איך שלום)

- Shalom, matai yotzet hatisa leRoma? (שלום, מתי יוצאת הטיסה לרומא)

- BeShmoneh BaBoker. (בשמונה בבוקר)

- Me'Eizeh Sha'ar? (מאיזה שער)

- Hi yotzet mi-sha'ar D21. (21ד משער יוצאת היא)

- Todah raba giveret. (תודה רבה גברת)

- Bavakasha, tisa ne'ima. (בבקשה תיסה נעימה)

Part 2

Traveling by taxi, bus, or train.

This part of the chapter is about traveling inside cities or in between cities.   It is best to know how to read Hebrew so you don't get lost even though many train and bus stations have signs in English to help you navigate.   But it's still better to know some Hebrew so you know can give basic directions.   I suggest knowing how to give directions because it will save you much time and money. In cities in Israel, you'll probably use the bus to get around, although you might use the train to travel between certain cities. Taxis are a great way to work on your Hebrew, but the drivers might be more interested in practicing their English.   Plus, they love to try to take advantage of tourists!   But if you don't mind, you can learn a lot about the culture and maybe even some history! Here are some of the phrases that will help you get around.

Cultural Note: One of the great things about Israel is the taxi-riding culture. It's entirely acceptable to haggle with the driver over the fare.   I recommend doing this before getting in the taxi.   Just keep in mind that is more the case in Jerusalem.   When I lived in Jerusalem, I did this all the time and had a ball doing so.   In other places in Israel, however, it's not so easy to haggle.   Taxi drivers will either give you a straight fare or insist on using the meter.

Taxi Vocabulary

Where are we going?	Le'an magi'im (לאן מגיעים)
I'm going to...	Ani Magi'a le... (אני מגיע ל)
At the stoplight, turn right/left	Ba'Ramzor, tifneh yemina/smola (תפנה ברמזור, בָּרמזור שמאלה/ימינה)
You can stop here.	Ta'atzor Po. (פה תעצר)
Here on the right/left	Po al ha-yamin/smol (שמאל/הימין על פה)
How much do I owe you?	Kama Ya'aleh li? (כמה יעלה לי)

*As I mentioned in the intro, verbs in Hebrew change constantly because of the root system and tense.   These are called **conjugations**. I will also show the conjugation in Hebrew in this circumstance for clarity purposes.   I will continue doing this until the end of the book.   **Note:**   The word for *to go* varies by method of transportation.   By car, train or bus the verb is *LaSu'a* and by plane it is *LaTus*.   The conjugations stay the same although the verb for to travel by car has an extra letter that doesn't appear in the infinitive form *LaSu'a*.   The word here, **LaLechet**, is generally used to denote travel by foot, i.e, walking.

* Below is the present tense conjugation of the verb: *LaLechet- to go* (ללכת)

Lalechet (ללכת)- to go

Ani **Holech** (אני הולך) ------- **I go**

Atah **Holech** (הולך אני)(masc.)/At **Holechet** (הולכת את) (fem.) -------**you go**

Hu **Holech** (הוא הולך)/ Hi **Holechet** (היא הולכת) ———**he, she goes; it goes**

Anachnu **Holchim** (אנחנו הולכים)(masc.)/Anachnu **Holcho**t (אנחנו הולכות)(fem.) ——— **we go**

Atem **Holchim** ((אתם הולכים)masc.)/Aten **Holchot** (אתן הולכות) (fem.). -------**you all go**

Hem **Holchim** (הולכים המ) /Hen **Holchot** (הולכות הן) ————-**They go**

Hazara!

Put the verb *Lalechet* in the correct form.

1. Ani _____   LaMakolet bechol boker..

2. Le'An atem _____ ?

3. Hu lo _____ laBank lehamir kesef?

4. ¿ Anachnu _____ bemehirut ki anachnu me'umcharim.

5. Lama atah _____ begeshem velo rochev al otobus?

Match the Phrases

6. Ta'atzor po.——————————————a. Here on the right.

7. Le'n anachnu magi'im?----------------------b. How much do I owe you?

8. Baramzor tifneh smola----------------------c. You can stop here

9. Po al hayamin--------------------d. Where are we going?

10. Kama ahi chayav lecha? --------------------e. At the stoplight, turn left.

Bus and Train Vocabulary

The bus/train station	Tachanat Otobus/Rakevet (תהנת רכבת)
Bus stop	Tachanat Otobus (אוטובוס תחנת)

When does the next train leave for…?	Matai HaRakevet Haba'ah le…? (מתי הרכבת הבאה ל)
I would like a one way ticket	Ani rotzeh kivvum echad (אני רוצה כיוון אחד)
Round trip ticket	Haloch VeChazor (הלוך וחזור)
Which platform does the train leave from?	Me'ezah ratzif harakevet yotzet (מאיזה רציף הרכבת יוצאת)
Do I need to change trains?	Ha'im ahi tzarich lhachlif rakevot? (האם אני צריך להחליף רכבות)
To get on…	La'alot (לעלות)
To get off..	Lered/Leredet (לרד/ת)

*Verb Conjugation

LaTzet (לצאת)- To leave

Ani **Yotzeh** (אני יוצא) ------- **I go**
Atah **Yozteh** (יוצא אני)(masc.)/At **Yotzet** (יוצאת את) (fem.) -------**you go**
Hu **Yotzeh** (הוא יוצא)/ Hi **Yotzet** (היא יוצאת) ———**he, she goes; it goes**
Anachnu **Yotz'im** (אנחנו יוצאים/יוצאות) ——— **we go**
Atem **Yotz'im** ((אתם יוצאים)masc.)/Aten **Yotz'ot** (אתן יוצאות) (fem.). -------**you all go**
Hem **Yotz'im** (יוצאים הם) /Hen **Yotz'ot** (יוצאות הן) ————**They go**

Ex: Hu yotzeh me'avoda beshesh = He leaves work at 6

Hazara!

Put the verb *LaTzet* in the correct form.

11. Ani _____ La'Avoda basha'ah sheva vachetzi.

12. Matai _____ ha-otobus leTel Aviv?

13. Hu _____ bli me'il.

14. Hem _____ al otobus shemagi'a le'Afula.

15. Hi _____ mehabayit besha'ah meuchar.

Translate to English

- Boker tov.   Eych ani yachol la'azor? (בוקר טוב, איך אני יכול לעזור)

- Matai haRakevet haba'ah leModi'in? (מתי הרכבת הבאה למודיעין)

- HaRakevet harishona yotzet beshesh baboker. (הרכבת הראשונה יוצאת בשש בבוקר)

- Todah.   Ani rotzeh kartis haloch vechazor leModi'in.
(תודה. אני רוצה כרטיס הלוך וחזור למודיעין)

- Beseder. (בסדר)

- Me'Ezeh ratzif hi yotzet? (מאיזה רציף היא יוצאת)

- Ratzif shesh. (רציף שש)

- Todah. (תודה)

- Bevakasha, nesi'a ne'ima. (בבקשה, נסיעה נעימה)

Chapter 12: Part 1 Answers

Fill in the blank with the word from the word bank

Isuf Mizvadot ----- Yotzeh
Terminal Bet ----Yagia
BaMatos----- Sde Te'ufa

1.   Ani Michapeset Isuf Mizvadot.
2. Matai Yotzeh HaTisa?
3.   Terminal Bet Nimtza BeTzad Hasheni shel Hasde Te'ufa.
4. Tasti LeNew York baMatos Shel Delta.
5. HaTisa yihyeh me'uchar veyagia beshtaim baboker.

Match the Vocabulary

6. Ya'ad --------------------e. Destination
7. Tisa Ne'ima--------------------c. Have a good trip
8. Matos————————a.Airplane
9. Meches ----------------------b. Customs
10. Kartis Tisa-------------------d. Ticket

Translation

- Shalom, Eych ahi yachol la'azor?
- Shalom, matai yotzeh hatisa leRoma?
- BeShmoneh BaBoker.
- Me'Eizeh Sha'ar?
- Hi yotzet mi-sha'ar D21.
- Todah raga giveret.
- Bavakasha, tisa ne'ima.

- Hi, how can I help you?
- Hi, when does the flight to Roma leave?
- It takes off at 8 AM.
- What gate does it leave from?
- From gate D21
- Thank you, ma'am
- Your welcome, bon voyage!

Chapter 12: Part 2 Answers

Put the verb *Lalechet* in the correct form.

1. Ani **Holechet**   LaMakolet bechol boker..

2. Le'An atem **Holchim** ?

3. Hu lo **holech** laBank lehamir kesef?

4. ¿ Anachnu **Holchim** bemehirut ki anachnu me'umcharim.

5. Lama atah **Holech** begeshem velo rochev al otobus?

Match the Phrases

6. Ta'atzor po.———————————— c. You can stop here

7. Le'n anachnu magi'im?----------------------d. Where are we going?

8. Baramzor tifneh smola----------------------e. At the stoplight, turn left.

9. Po al hayamin---------------------a. Here on the right.

10. Kama ahi chayav lecha? --------------------b. How much do I owe you?

Put the verb *LaTzet* in the correct form

11. Ani **Yotzeh** La'Avoda basha'ah sheva vachetzi.

12. Matai   **Yotzeh** ha-otobus leTel Aviv?

13. Hu   **Yotzeh**   bli me'il.

14. Hem Yotz'im al otobus shemagi'a le'Afula.

15. Hi yotzet mehabayit besha'ah meuchar.

Translation

- Boker tov.   Eych ani yachol la'azor?
- Matai haRakevet haba'ah leModi'in?
- HaRakevet harishona yotzet beshesh baboker.
- Todah.   Ani rotzeh kartis haloch vechazor leModi'in
- Beseder.
- Me'Ezeh ratzif hi yotzet?
- Ratzif shesh.
- Todah.

- Bevakasha, nesi'a ne'ima.

- Good morning, how can I help you?
- What time does the next train leave for Modi'in?
- The first train leaves at 6AM.
- Thank you. I would like a round trip ticket to Modi'n.
- Okay.
- Which platform does the train leave from?
- platform 6.
- Okay, thank you.
- Your welcome, have a good trip.

Chapter 13
Finding a place to stay

?לערב חדר להזמין אפשר

In Israel, you don't have to only stay at hotels by the Tel Aviv beach.   There are also hostels with nice accommodations as well as smaller motels and *Tzimmers*, basically bed and breakfasts that you can rent for several days at a time. Almost all of these places will have the comforts of home.   Just keep in mind that hot water usually comes from a *dud shemesh* (sun water boiler) and may not get to the temperature you want during the winter.   Here's a list of words that should help you book a room at your new destination. Enjoy your stay!

Hotel Vocabulary

I would like to reserve a room for one/two people.	Ani rotzeh lehazmin cheder le'echad/shnei anashim. (אני רוצה להזמין הדר לאהד/לשני אנשים)
How much does it cost per night?	Kama ya'aleh la-kol layla? (לילה לכל יעלה כמה)
For how many people?	Lekama anashim? (לכמה אנשים)
For how many nights?	Lekama laylot? (לילות לכמה)
Para una noche/dos noches	Lelayla echat/leshtey leylot (לילות לשתי/אחת ללילה)
With a double bed.	Im mitah kfula (עם מיטה כפולה)
With two single beds	Im shtei mitot (עם שתי מיטות)
I'm sorry, we are full.	Ani mitzta'er, anachnu melay'im (אני מצטער אנהנו מלאים)
I have a reservation.	Yesh li hazmanah. (יש לי הזמנה)

Do you have wi-fi?	Yesh lachem wifi? (יש לכם wifi?)

Hazara!

Match the Phrases

1. I'm sorry we are full------------------------a. Lekama laylot?

2. For how many people?---------------------b. Yesh li hazmana.

3. I have a reservation.-------------------------c. Kama lekol layla?

4. For how many nights?----------------------d. Le kama anashim?

5. How much is it per night?------------------e. Ani Mitzta'er, anachnu melay'im

Translate to English

- Erev Tov. (ערב טוב)

- Erev tov.   Eych ani yachol la'azor? (ערב טוב. איך אני יכול לעזור?)

- Ani rotzeh lehazmin cheder le'echad. (אני רוצה להזמין חדר לאחד)

- LeKama laylot? (לכמה לילות?)

- LeShavua. (לשבוע)

- Beseder. (בסדר)

- Kama oleh lekol layla? (כמה לכל לילה?)

   Me'ah dollar la'erev, aval yeah mivtza achshav ve'atah yachol lisha'er shavua le arba me'ot dollar.
   (מאה דולר לערב, אבל יש מבצע עכשול ואתה יכול לישאר שבוע לארבע מאות דולר)

- VeYesh lachem wi-fi? (ויש לכם ווי–פיי?)

- Betach. (בטח)

   Todah. (תודה)

Chapter 13 Answers

Match the Phrases

1. I'm sorry we are full-----------------------e. Ani Mitzta'er, anachnu melay'im
2. For how many people?--------------------d. Lekama anashim?
3. I have a reservation.-----------------------b. Yesh li hazmana.
4. For how many nights?---------------------a. Lekama laylot?
5. How much is it per night?------------------c. Kama lekol layla?

Translation

- Erev Tov.
- Erev tov.   Eych ani yachol la'azor?
- Ani rotzeh lehazmin cheder le'echad.
- LeKama laylot?
- LeShavua.
- Beseder.
- Kama oleh lekol layla?
   Me'ah dollar la'erev, aval yeah mivtzah achshav ve'atah yachol lisha'er
   shavua lematayim dollar.
- VeYesh lachem wi-fi?
- Betach.
   Todah.

- Good evening.
- Good evening, ma'am, how can I help you?
- I would like to reserve a room for one person.
- For how many nights?
-- For a week.
- Okay.
- How much is it per night?
- 100 dollars per night, but we have a sale right now where you can stay for a week for 400 dollars.
- And do you have wi-fi?
- Certainly.
- Thank you.

SECTION 3
GETTING TO KNOW EACH OTHER

Chapter 14
Describing Things, People & Places

?זה איך

This chapter starts a new subject.   Until now, we focused on getting you around and how to handle local life.   Now we're going to shift to talking to people so you can make friends.   This chapter should give you all the tools you need to have a basic conversation about yourself.   Here are some useful words for describing yourself and everything around you.

Description Vocabulary

tall	gavoha (גבוה)
short	namuch/a (נמוכה/נמוך)
fat	shamen/shmena (שמנה/שמן)
thin	razeh/ah (רזה)
pretty	yafe/a (יפה)
handsome	yafe/a (יפה)
cute	nechmad/a (ה/נחמד)
hair	se'ar (שער)
short (length)	ketzar/a (ה/קצר)
long	aroch/aruka (ה/ארוך)
big	gadol/gedola (ה/גדול)
small	katan/ketana (ה/קטן)
strong	chazak/a (ה/חזק)
ugly	mecho'ar/a (ה/מכוער)
old	zaken/zkena (ה/זקן)
young	tza'ir/a (ה/צעיר)

***Note:**   The masculine/feminine differences in Hebrew should be more obvious with this list.   The words ending with *a* are feminine.   This is one the easiest ways to know which set of conjugations to use. Remember that you must match the adjective with the gender of the noun.   If you get confused, don't worry - most people get confused, occasionally even Israelis!

Description Phrases and More Vocabulary

What's it like?	Eych zeh? (איך זה)
What does he/she look like?	Eych hu nir'eh/hi nir'ah? (איך הוא/היא נראה)
He is…/She is …	hu…./hi…. (…הוא/היא)
I am…	Ani… (…אני)
What color is his/her hair?	Aizeh tzeva sa'ar yeah lo/lah? (איזה צבע שער יש לו/לה)
His/her hair is….	sa'ar shelo tzeva…. (שער שלו צבע..)
Does she have long hair?	Yesh la se'ar aruka? (יש לה שער ארוכה)
He has short hair.	Yesh lo se'ar katzar (יש לו שער קצר)
blonde	blondini/t (בלונדיני/ת)
brunette	Shecharchoret (שחרחרת)
red headed	gingi/t (ג׳ינג׳י/ת)

*Verb Conjugation

<u>to be</u> <u>להיות</u>

Like English, the verb *To be* is not expressed   in Hebrew.   Rather it is contained in the present tense verb itself.   It does appear in the present and future tenses.   Thus, below are two conjugation charts, one for past tense and one for future.   **Note:** The conjugation charts work for all verbs and almost all verb forma.

Past Tense Verb - להיות (To Be)

Person	Masculine	Feminine
1st person - I was	Hayiti (הייתי)	Hayiti (הייתי)
2nd person - You were	Hayita (היית)	Hayita (היית)
3rd person - He/she/it was	Haya (היה)	Hayta (היתה)
1st person plural - We were	Hayeenu (היינו)	Hayeenu (היינו)
2nd person plural - You were	Hayeetem (הייתם)	Hayeeten (הייתן)
3rd person plural - They were	Hayu (היו)	Hayu (היו)

In regards to past tense, the form here applies to all verbs.   Note that the form is root xxx + suffix.   This means the the past tense is expressed by the suffix. For example, if you wanted to say *I walked*, the word in Hebrew for walk is *Halach* (הלךְ). You add the suffix -ti (תי) to the end of the word for *Halachti* (הלכתי).   Verb forms and the root system of Hebrew will be discussed in depth at the end of the book.

Future Tense Verb - להיות (To Be)

Person	Masculine	Feminine
1st person - I will be	Ehyeh (אהיה)	Ehyeh (אהיה)
2nd person - You will be	Tihyeh (תהיה)	Tihyee (תהיי)
3rd person - He/she/it will be	Yihyeh (יהיה)	Tihyeh (תהיה)
1st person plural - We will be	Nihyeh (נהיה)	Nihyeh (נהיה)

Person	Masculine	Feminine
2nd person plural - You will be	Tihyu (תהיו)	Tihyena (תהיינה)
3rd person plural - They will be	Yihyu (יהיו)	Yihyu (יהיו)

Hazara!

Put the verb *Lihiyot* in the correct form and translate the sentence.

1. _____ razeh im ani ratz bekol yom--

_____

2. Hu _____ babyit etmol.------

_____

3. Efo _____ mahar?-----------

_____

4. _____ lah se'ar tzahov im hi yoshevet bachof.-------

_____

5. Hee _____ bamisada batzahorayim. -------------

_____

Translate the   Phrases

1. Eych hu nir'eh? --------------------------

_____

2. Hi nemucha razah veyafah meod.------------

_____

3. Eitzeh tzevah se'ar yesh lo?--------------

_____

4. Yesh lah af katan.————

_____

5. HaIm yesh lo se'ar aroch?------------------

_____

6. Hu chazak.————

_____

*Below I will list some words to describe your emotions. You should use forms of the verb *estar* to talk about your emotions.

Ex: estoy contenta.=I am happy.

Emotion Vocabulary

How do you feel?	Eych ata/at margish/a?
I feel...	Ani margish/a
Happy	Same'ach/smecha
Sad	Atzuv/a
Tired	Ayef/a
Excited	Mitragesh/et
Bored	Mesha'amem/a
Angry	Ko'es/Ko'esa
Nervous	Atzbani/t
Calm	Ragu'a
Busy	Asuk/a
Scared	Poched/Pocheda

Match the Vocabulary

1. happy——————————————————————a. Ko'es
2. excited————————————————————b. Atzbani
3. nervous——————————————————— c. Merugash
4. bored——————————————————————d. Ayef
5. angry——————————————————————e. Meshua'am
6. sad ————————————————————————f. Poched
7. calm—————————————————————g. Atzuv
8.   busy——————————————————————h. Sameach
9. scared————————————————————i. Asuk
10. tired———————————————————————j. Ragu'a

Chapter 14 Answers

Put the verb *Lehiyot* in the correct form and translate the sentence.

1. <u>Ehyeh</u> razeh im ani ratz bekol yom—————-<u>I will be thin if I run every day.</u>

2. Hu <u>Haya</u> babyit etmol.——————————-<u>He was at home yesterday.</u>

3. Efo <u>Tihyeh</u> mahar?——————————-—-<u>Where will you be tomorrow?</u>

4.   <u>Tihyeh</u> lah se'ar tzahov im hi holechet lachof.—<u>She'll have blonde hair if she goes to the beach.</u>

5. Hee <u>Hayta</u> bamisada batzahorayim. —-———-<u>She was at the restaurant in the afternoon.</u>

Translate the   Phrases

1. Eych hu nir'eh? ———————————<u>What does he look like?</u>

2. Hi nemucha razah veyafah meod.————<u>She's short, thin and very pretty.</u>

3. Eitzeh tzevah se'ar yesh lo?———————<u>What color hair does he have?</u>

4. Yesh lah af katan.————————————<u>She has a small nose.</u>

5. Halm yesh lo se'ar aroch?————————<u>Does he have long hair?</u>

6. Hu chazak.————————————————<u>He is strong.</u>

Match the Vocabulary

1. happy——————————————————h. Sameach
2. excited—————————————————— c. Merugash
3. nervous————————————————— b. Atzbani
4. bored——————————————————e. Meshua'am
5. angry——————————————————a. Ko'es
6. sad ——————————————————g. Atzuv
7. calm—————————————————————j. Ragu'a
8.   busy—————————————————— i. Asuk
9. scared—————————————————f. Poched
10. tired——————————————————d. Ayef

Chapter 15
We Are a Family! (Vocabulary & Phrases)

כמה אחים יש לך?

Now we'll talk about the family.   In generally Israelis consider everyone to be family, which sometimes explains their behavior - you're a cousin, so who cares if I'm a bit pushy?   We're family!   After this chapter, you should be able to talk about your siblings, cousins and other family members.   Families are very close in Israel and constantly get together.   Here's the vocabulary you'll need to be able to speak about your family.

Family vocabulary and phrases

How many siblings do you have?	Kama achim yesh lecha/lach? (כמה אחים יש לך?)
I have 3 siblings.	Yesh li shlosha achim. (This depends on gender. If you have only sisters you will use the word for sisters and the feminine form of the number. Otherwise, use the masculine form.) (יש לי שלושה אחים)
Brother	Ach/im (אח/ים)
Sister	Achot/Achayot (אחיות/אחות)
Mom	Imma (אמא)
Dad	Abba (אבא)
Mother	Imma (אמא)
Father	Abba (אבא)
grandpa/grandma	Saba/Savta (סבתא/סבא)
cousin (female/male)	Bat Dod/Ben Dod (דוד בן/דוד בת)

husband/wife	Ba'al/Isha (אשה/בעל)
son/daughter	Ben/Bat (בת/בן)
uncle/aunt	Dod/Doda (דודה/דוד)
Pet	Chaya Michmad (חיה מחמד/חיות מחמד)
Dog	Kelev (כלב)
Cat	Chatul (חתול)
Older	Yoter Zaken (זקן יותר)
Younger	Yoter Tza'ir (צעיר יותר)
Adult	Mevugar (מבוגד)
Great-grandfather/grandmother	Saba Raba/Savta Raba (סבא רבה/סבתא רבה)

* Remember that the adjective comes after noun.

younger brother = Ach katan

older sister = Achot gedola

You can say *Yoter Zaken* for saying someone is older, but the colloquial form is *Mevugar Yoter*.

*Verb Conjugation

Note: From this point onward I will be putting all verb conjugations into chart format with present tenses. All you have to do is memorize the chart!

Yesh (יש)— to have

Person	Masculine	Feminine
1st - I have	Yesh Li (יש לי)	Yesh Li (יש לי)
2nd person - You have	Yesh Lecha (יש לך)	Yesh Lach (יש לך)
3rd person - He/She/it has	Yesh Lo (לו)	Yesh Lah (לה)

Person	Masculine	Feminine
1st plural - We have	Yesh Lanu (לָנוּ)	Yesh Lanu (לָנוּ)
2nd plural - You have	Yesh Lachem (לָכֶם)	Yesh Lachen (לָכֶן)
3rd plural - They have	Yesh Lahem (לָהֶם)	Yesh Lahen (לָהֶן)

*It's useful to know the possessive pronouns in order to talk about family, so you can say – *my* mom, *his* sister, *her* grandma, etc.

Possessive Pronouns

My	Sheli (שלי)
Your	Shelcha, Shelach (שלך)
His or Her	Shelo/Shela (שלה,שלו)
Our	Shelanu (שלנו)
Yours (Plural)	Shelachem, Shelachen (שלכם/ן)
Their	Shelahem, Shelahen (שלהם/ן)

*Notice you that possessives also match gender and number.
Ex: My brother = Ach Sheli
My siblings = Achim Sheli
Our grandma = Savta Shelanu

Note: There are also shorter possessives that consist of adding a single letter suffix to the end of a word.   They consist of the final syllables in chart for *Shel* above.   It considered to be high level Hebrew to use them instead of the chart above.

Another important note: The possessive suffixes also double as past tense markers that denote who is performing the action.   Thus, *Dibar**nu** im David* means "We spoke with David".   This was explained before but I repeat it now so you don't get confused.   The best way to avoid that confusion, is context. Context will tell you whether the suffix is a tense marker, possessive or something else altogether.

Hazara!

Put the possessive verb *Yesh l-* in the correct form and translate the sentence.

1. _____Shalosh Achim.

_____

2. Slicha, efo _____ sherutim?

_____

3. _____ lah rak achim?

_____

4. _____ le-ach sheli se'ar adom._____

5. _____ la__ chatul, kelev vetzipor._____

Match the Vocabulary

1. Yoter Zaken--a. grandma

2. Abba--b. pet

3. Doda--c. older

4. Yoter Tza'ir--d. aunt

5. Saba--e. dad

6. Dod--f. grandpa

7. Chaya Michamad--g. husband

8. Ba'al --h. wife

9. Isha--i. younger

10. Savta--j.uncle

Put the possessive pronoun in the correct form

1. (My) Saba_____ lo zaken me'od.

2. (His) Achot _____ yafah u'me'od tza'ira.

3. (Our) Kelev vechatul _____ chachamim aval atzlanim.

4. (Your) Yesh le-Abba _____ achim oh achayot?

5. (Their) Ach _____ yoter tza'ir.

Write about your family following the example

Yesh li shlosha achim.   Achot sheli bat 34 ve kor'im la leah.   Hi gara beNew York.   Hi lo nesu'a.   Yesh li ach yoter tza'ir vekor'im lo yuval.   Korim le-ishto malka.   Hem garim beLos Angeles.   Imma sheli korim la Nora ve-Abba, shem shelo Matityahu.   Horim shell garim beTzafon Tel Aviv.   Ve-ach hakatan shelanu, korim lo eldad.   Hu nimtzah baShanghai velomed Sinit.

(יש לי שלושה אחים. אחות שלי בת 34 וקוראים לה לאה. היא גרה בניו יורק. היא לא נשואה. יש לי אח צעיר יותר וקוראים לו יובל.   קוראים לאשתו מלכה. הם גרים בלוס אנגלס. אמא סלי קוראימ לאבא ,שם נורה לה אביב. מתיהו שלו גרים שלי הורים בצפון תל ואח. קטן שלנו קוראים לו אלדד.
הוא נמצא בשאנגהאי ולומד סינית.)

Chapter 15 Answers

Put the verb *tener* in the correct form and translate the sentence.

1. Yesh Li Shalosh Achim. _____ I have three siblings.
2. Slicha, efo Yesh sherutim? ___ Excuse me, where is there a bathroom?
3. Yesh lah rak achim? _____ She only has brothers?
4. Yesh le-ach sheli se'ar adom.___ My brother has red hair.
5. Yesh Lanu chatul, kelev vetzipor. _We have a cat, dog and bird.

Match the Vocabulary

1. Yoter Zaken--c. older
2. Abba--e. dad
3. Doda--d. aunt
4. Yoter Tza'ir---i. younger
5. Saba--f. grandpa
6. Dod--j.uncle
7. Chaya Michamad-------------------------------------b. pet
8. Ba'al --g. husband
9. Isha--h. wife
10. Savta---a. grandma

Put the possessive pronoun in the correct form

1 1. (My) Saba sheli lo zaken me'od.

2. (His) Achot shelo yafah u'me'od tza'ira.

3. (Our) Kelev vechatul shelanu chachamim aval atzlanim.

4. (Your) Yesh le-Abba shelcha achim oh achayot?

5. (Their) Ach Shelahem yoter tza'ir.

Write about your family following the example

Various possible answers.

Person	Masculine	Feminine
1st - I love	Ani Ohev (אני אוהב)	Ani Ohevet (אני אוהבת)
2nd person - You have	Atah Ohev (אתה אוהב)	At Ohevet (את אוהבת)
3rd person - He/She/it has	Hu Ohev (הוא אוהב)	Hee Ohevet (היא אוהבת)
1st plural - We have	Anachnu Ohavim (אנחנו אוהבים)	Anachnu Ohavot (אנחנו אוהבות)
2nd plural - You have	Atem Ohavim (אתם אוהבים)	Aten Ohavot (אתן אוהבות)
3rd plural - They have	Hem Ohavim (הם אוהבים)	Hen Ohavot (הן אוהבות)

Chapter 16
All work and no play makes Yuval a boring boy

מה המקצוע שלך?

Now that we are able to describe ourselves physically and discuss our family, we can talk about what we do, our career. It is something that we often talk about and sometimes unfortunately can consume our lives. In Latin American culture, they are often surprised at how work is such a big part of our lives. As I mentioned in the previous chapter, helping each other out as friends and family is often more important than one's individual career and success. In this chapter, you will learn some basic professions of our society.

Occupational vocabulary and phrases

What do you do?	Mah ha-miktzo'ah shelcha/shelach? (מה המקצוע שלך)
I am a teacher.	Ani moreh/morah. (מורה אני)
teacher	Moreh/Morah (מורה)
businessman/business woman	Ish Asakim (איש/אשה עסקים)
Doctor	Rofeh/Rofah (ה/רופא)
Nurse	Achot (אחות)
Lawyer	Orech/et Din (עורכ/ת דין)
Writer	Kotev/et (כותב/ת)
policeman	Shoter/et (שוטר/ת)
firefighter	Kaveh (כבה)
student	Student/it (talmid/a) (ית/סטודנט) (ה/תלמיד)
receptionist	mazkira (מזכיר/ה)
Waiter	Meltzar/it (ית/מלצר)
Cook	Ofeh/ah (אופה)

salesperson	Mocheret (מוכר/ת)
engineer	Mehandes/et (מהנדס/ת)

*By now, you can probably guess why most of the occupations end in either *o* or *a*

Ex: Orech Din = lawyer (male)
Orechet Din = lawyer (female)

* Hebrew differentiates between females and males much more often in its words. You notice when you say lawyer in English, you don't know the person's gender.   In Hebrew, you know immediately.

* The term for a student *Talmid* is the formal Hebrew term for a student.   It has been mostly replaced by the somewhat cringe-worthy English term.

Hazara!

Match the Vocabulary

1. Ish Asakim--------------------------------------a. police officer

2. Kaveh-----------------------------------b. nurse

3. Achot---------------------------------------c. doctor

4. Orech Din-------------------------------------d. businessman

5. Meltzar----------------------------------e. salesperson

6. Rofeh-----------------------------------f. waiter

7. Ofeh----------------------------------g. firefighter

8. Mocher-----------------------------------h. attorney

9. Shoter-----------------------------------i. engineer

10. Mehandes--j. cook

Put the correct form of the word according to gender.

1. Abba Shelo _____   (Rofeh/Rofah).

2. Ishti ovedet ke   _____ (Kotevs/Kotevet).

3. Hu haya _____ (Moreh/Moreh) BaTichon beNew York.

4. Achanu tzrichim _____ (Orech Din/Orechet Din) la'azor im ba'aya I'm ba'al dira shelanu.

5. Ani oved   ke _____   (Meltzar/Meltzarit). (Answer according to your gender)

Answer the following question about your occupation. Don't forget to answer according to your gender.

Mah HaMiktzo'ah Shelcha/Shelach?

_____

_

Chapter 16 Answers

Match the Vocabulary

1. Ish Asakim----------------------------d. businessman
2. Kaveh--------------------------------g. firefighter
3. Achot--------------------------------b. nurse
4. Orech Din----------------------------h. attorney
5. Meltzar------------------------------f. waiter
6. Rofeh--------------------------------c. doctor
7. Ofeh———————————j. cook
8. Mocher-------------------------------e. salesperson
9. Shoter-------------------------------a. police officer
10. Mehandes----------------------------i. engineer

Put the correct form of the word according to gender.

1. Abba Shelo <u>Rofeh</u>   (Rofeh/Rofah).

2. Ishti ovedet ke<u>Kotev</u> (Kotev/Kotevet).

3. Hu haya <u>Moreh</u> (Moreh/Moreh) BaTichon beNew York.

4. Achanu tzrichim <u>Orechet Din</u> (Orech Din/Orechet Din) la'azor im ba'aya I'm ba'al dira shelanu.

5. Ani oved   ke <u>answers will vary</u>   (Meltzar/Meltzarit). (Answer according to your gender)

Ma HaMiktzo'ah Shelcha?

<u>Answers will vary.</u>

Chapter 17
Hobbies (I Like to...)

?חפשי בזמן עושה אתה מה

Now you can talk about yourself, we can move on to hobbies.   Israelis often have the same hobbies as you, although they tend to have more in common with Europeans, especially in regards to sports.   Below you will find useful phrases to discuss hobbies and also an explanation of the verb *Ohev* so that you can talk about what you like.

Vocabulary to discuss your Hobbies

I like ...	Ani ohev....
I don't like	Ani lo ohev..
free time	Zman chofshi
play sports	lesachek sport
play videogames	lasechek mischakei video
travel	LaSo'a
read	Likro
go to the movies	LaLechet LeKolno'a
go to the beach	Lalechet lachof
watch TV	letzapot televizia
watch sports	letzapot mischakei sport
listen to music	lishmo'a musica
play an instrument	lenagen.....
ski	Ski
spend time with friends	Levalot zman Im chaverim

You will learn how all conjugations for verbs in the last section of this book.

There is no singular phrase for "playing sports" - what appears is what I've heard used.   People are actually more specific and name the sport they are referring to.

* The verb *Ohev- to like*. The verb actually means *to love*, but is used to mean *to like* as well.   Here are the conjugations for *Ohev* following the chart format it outlined earlier.

* If you want to say, *I don't like* simply add *lo* (לֹא) in front.

Ex: You don't like =   Atah lo ohev

He doesn't like = Hu lo ohev

* The affixes for plural and singular verbs here also are used to denote plural nouns as well as adjective.   *-ot* generally marks feminine words while *-im* marks masculine.   In addition, these will often match other parts of the sentence.   However, there are exceptions, like in all languages, so this rule is not universal.

Hazara!

Choose the correct answer

1. I like to go to the movies.

a. Ani lo ohev lalechet lakolno'a.--------------b. Ani ohevet lir'ot sratim.

c. Ani ohev lalechet lakolno'a.----------------d. Ani rotzeh lalechet lakolno'a.

2. Do you like to read?

a. Atah ohev lschot? --------------------b. Atah ohev likro?

c. At ohevet likro? ——————d. At lo ohevet likro?

3. I don't like to travel.

a. Ani ohev liso'a-------------- b. Ani ohev lso'a barakevet.

c. Ani lo yode'ah im ani rotzeh lasu'a------------------d. Ani lo ohev liso'a.

Match the Verb Phrases
1. Lalechet lachof---------------------------------a. Spend time with friends
2. letzapot mischakei sport----------------------b. Play video games
3. Levalot zman Im chaverim------------------ c. Watch sports.
4.   lesachek sport ----------------------------------- d. Go to the beach
5.   lasechek mischakei video------------------------------e. Play sports

Chapter 17 Answers

Choose the correct answer

1. I like to go to the movies.

d. Ani rotzeh lalechet lakolno'a.

2. Do you like to read?

c. At ohevet likro?

3. I don't like to travel.

d. Ani lo ohev liso'a.

Match the Verb Phrases

1. Lalechet lachof-------------------------------d. Go to the beach
2. letzapot mischakei sport————————— c. Watch sports.
3. Levalot zman Im chaverim------------------ a. Spend time with friends
4.   lesachek sport ------------------------------- e. Play sports
5.   lasechek mischakei video--------------------b. Play video games

SECTION 4
GRAMMAR SCHOOL

Chapter 18
To Be or Not to Be...

....השאלה זה, להיות לו או להיות

In the last section of this crash course we will discuss some of the difficult grammar topics of Hebrew in the simplest way possible.   As you probably know, languages cannot be translated word for word and often one word in one language can be communicated in more than one way depending on the situation. The infinitive in Hebrew is a way to express *to do x*.   It is also the easiest way to learn roots of words.   It can be complicated because of *Binyanim*, specific affixes that add aspect to verbs.   I will explain the infinitive below as well as how you can derive a wide range of words from a single root.

Infinitives

Infinitives always have the format of *Le + verb* in *x* verb structure.   In Hebrew this appears as follows: ל + פועל.   Below is chart of examples of infinitive formats of common verbs.

Verb in Hebrew	Pronunciation	Translation
לאכול	Le-Echol	To eat
לשתות	Li-shtot	To drink
לעמוד	La-amod	To stand
לשבת	La-Shevet	To sit
לישון	Li-shon	To sleep
ללמוד	Li-Lmod	To study

Verb Forms

Hebrew Form	English transcription	Aspect added	Example

פָּעַל	Pa'al	Active voice	Kafatz - He jumped
נִפְעַל	Nif'al	Passive	Nishbar - it broke
פִּעֵל	Pi'el	Intensity	Limed - He taught
פּוּעַל	Pu'al	Passive only, not commonly used	Me'unyan - interested
הִפְעִיל	Hif'il	Active voice	Hichtiv - He dictated
הוּפְעַל	Huf'al	Passive, only really used as a present participle	Mukar - Known
הִתְפַּעֵל	Hitpa'el	Reflexive	Histaper - to get a haircut

The structure for verbs in the chart above uses the root Pa'al, to do, as a fill in. The letters are merely placeholders. You can plug in any three letter and get some kind of word.

Example: If you took the verb Pa'al and plugged in the root spelled Shin, Tav, Heh - Shatah (שתה) in place of the holders Peh, Ayin, Lamed - you now have the word for *He Drank*.

Word Derivation

We've now reached the most interesting part of Hebrew: Word derivation. As I've said before, Hebrew is built around a three letter root system and a series of affixes - suffixes, affixes and even circumflexes (those which frame a root) to create its vocabulary. We will look at that presently, using one or two different roots. At this point, we're about to use a lot of words in Hebrew to show the derivation. Don't worry! I will transcribe everything so you won't get lost.

Root form: Lamad (למד)

The root **Lamad** is associated with study, teaching or learning.   From this word, you can derive the following verbs using the verb formats above:

Lilamed (ללמד) - to teach
Lilmod (ללמוד) - to study

We can derive the following nouns as well:
Talmid (תלמיד) - Student
Lemida (למידה) - Learning
Melamed (מלמד) - Teacher (This is term that was used to refer to a Torah teacher in Pre-War II Europe)
Melumad (מלומד) - Scholar

Root form: Katav (כתב)
The word **Katav** has everything to do with writing.   Again, using the charts above, we can derive the following verbs:

Lichtov (לכתוב) - to write
Hichtiv (הכתיב) - he dictated
Hitkatev (התכתב) - he corresponded with

We can also derive a ton of words from this root.   Here are some that will be quite useful:
Hitkatvut (התכתבות) - correspondence
Kotev (כותב) - a writer
Ketovet (כתובת) - address
Ketubah (כתובה) - a traditional Jewish marriage document
Ketuvit (כתובית) - Subtitles
Ketav Yad (כתב יד) - Manuscript

Note: I highly recommend looking at all verbs in chart format.   This will make the relationships between words so much clearer.

Hazara!

See if you can remember how to use infinitives below

Ani rotzeh _____ (Root: Beeker, to visit) Savta machar.
Ani Tzarich _____ (Root: Zachar, to remember) darkon sheli.

Root: Achal, to eat _____

Lo _____ (Root: Zaman, form Hif'il, invite) yoter midai anashim.

Try your hand at deriving words from a noun (Feel free to use a dictionary for help).

1. Root: Zachar, to remember (זכר):

_____

_____

2. Root: Rasham, to list (רשם):

_____

_____

3. Root: Rachatz, to wash (רחץ):

_____

_____

4. Root: Shavar to break (שבר):

_____

_____

Chapter 18 Answers

See if you can remember how to use infinitives below

Ani rotzeh **levaker** (Root: Biker, to visit) Savta machar.
Ani Tzarich **lizkor** (Root: Zachar, to remember) darkon sheli.
Lo **lehazmin** (Root: Zaman, form Hif'il, invite) yoter midai anashim.

Try your hand at deriving words from a noun.
1. Root: Zachar, to remember (זכר): Lizkor - to remember, zikaron - memory, hizkir - mention, azkara -anniversary of a loved one's death
2. Root: Rasham, to list (רשם): Reshima - list, lirshom - to list, marshal - prescription
3. Root: Rachatz, to wash (רחץ): Lirchotz - to wash, lehitrachetz - to wash one's self, rechitza - washing,
4. Root: Shavar to break (שבר): Lishbor - to break, shiber- he shattered, shevarim - broken pieces (Also a sound made by the Shofar during the Jewish new year), shever - hope, shavrir - fragment

Chapter 19
Conjugating Verbs

We've now reached the most confusing part of Hebrew: Verb conjugations. We've discussed this briefly in other contexts but now we will explain it in depth. In English, it's fairly simple: *I eat, I ate, I will eat.* In Hebrew, present tense has four different changes alone. Adding in future and past adds another fifteen to twenty changes! I will show you, in charts, the full conjugations for verbs using the verb *To Eat* as an example.

Note: you will just have to memorize the charts. This is the simplest way to learn to use verb conjugations in Hebrew.

Step one: Remove Lamed
Step two: Plug verb into chart. That's it!

Past Tense Verb - לאכל (To Eat)

Person	Masculine	Feminine
1st - I ate	Ani Achalti (אני אכלתי)	Ani Achalti (אני אכלתי)
2nd - You ate	Atah Achalta (אתה אכלת)	At Achalt (את אכלת)
3rd - He/She/It ate	Hu Achal (הוא אכל)	Hee Achla (היא אכלה)
1st Plural - We ate	Anachnu Achalnu (אנחנו אכלנו)	Anachnu Achalnu (אנחנו אכלנו)
2nd Plural - You ate	Atem Achaltem (אתם אכלתם)	Aten Achalten (אתן אכלתן)
3rd Plural - They ate	Hem Achlu (הם אכלו)	Hen Achlu (הן אכלו)

Present Tense Verbs

Person	Masculine	Feminine
1st - I eat	Ani Ochel (אני אוכל)	Ani Ochelet (אני אוכלת)
2nd - You eat	Ani Ochel (אני אוכל)	Ani Ochelet (אני אוכלת)
3rd - He/She/It eats	Ani Ochel (אני אוכל)	Ani Ochelet (אני אוכלת)

Person	Masculine	Feminine
1st Plural - We eat	Anachnu Ochlim (אנחנו אוכלים)	Anachnu Ochlim (אנחנו אוכלים)
2nd Plural - You eat	Atem Ochlim (אתם אוכלים)	Aten Ochlot (אתן אוכלות)
3rd Plural - They eat	Hem Ochlim (הם אוכלים)	Hen Ochlot (הן אוכלות)

Future Tense

Person	Masculine	Feminine
1st - I will eat	Ani Eh-ehchol (אני אאכל)	Ani Eh-ehchol (אני אאכל)
2nd - You will eat	Atah Tochal (אתה תאכל)	At Tochali (את תאכלי)
3rd He/She/It will eat	Hu Yochal (הוא יאכל)	Hee Tochal (היא תאכל)
1st Plural - We will eat	Anachnu Nochal (אנחנו נאכל)	Anachnu Nochal (אנחנו נאכל)
2nd Plural - You will eat	Atem Tochlu (אתם תאכלו)	Aten Tochalna (אתן תאכלנה)
3rd Plural - They will eat	Hem Yochlu (הם יאכלו)	Hen Yochlu (הן יאכלו)

As stated before, Hebrew is built on a three letter root system and a series of affix patterns. The patterns make the language simple to learn and they are your greatest asset when learning the language. I repeat this because in Hebrew you have numerous affixes that attach to the beginning and end of words so that you can say an entire phrase with one word. You sometimes end up with several affixes framing a complex form verb.

Example: the verb *LeHitkale'ach* (להתקלח), to shower. This verb is in the *Hitpa'el* (התפעל) verb form, which is one of the longer verb patterns. If you wanted to say *I will shower*, the word is *Etkale'ach* (אתקלח). In this word, you simply drop the Heh (ה) at the beginning of the verb and add the future tense prefix. Note that this is not typically the case and you would simply add the affix.

However, if you wanted to say *When I will shower*, the word is now *KeSheEtkaleach* (כ–ש–אתקלח).   The Kaf prefix literally means *Like* and the Shin is *When*.   The two combine to mean "*when ___*".   In this case you've taken the verb, added tense and person affixes and then added two additional affixes to create a four-word English phrase in one word.   This is important to know because you can typically shorten phrases by using Hebrew affixes.

Examples: *In the house* - Babayit (בבית).   Ba = in the, Bayit = home

Thus you can see how the verb patterns make building verbs and phrases simple. In the first example, all we did was drop one letter from the verb, then add an affix.   Sounds simple.   The second example, we just added affixes after dropping one letter.   This is much simpler than having to construct phrases consisting of several words in English or any other language.   If you understand this chapter and the previous one, you've just figured out the simplest way to learn all of the languages in the Semitic language family that includes Arabic, Aramaic, Amharic and Chadic.   That's because they all function in the same way!

Hazara!

Using the charts as a guide, try creating verbs in different tenses in the sentences below.   Also translate the sentence. (Note: I have given you the root, definition, conjugation and tense.   It's up to you to figure out the proper form)

1. Lifnei chodesh ani _____   (Tas (fly, past tense) li Tel-Aviv.
_____

2.   Atah _____ (Halach, you, go, future tense) le'Misada machar?
_____

3. Anachnu _____ (Shatah, drink, we) mayim me'od karim.
_____

4.   Mi_____   (Shachach, forgot, past tense) darkon shelahem
bamatos? _____

5. Ani   _____   (lamad, learn, present, I) Sefaradit veTzarfartit ba-
Universita.
_____

Create a chart of your own for the verb *Lavash,* to wear, for past, present and future tenses.

Chapter 19 Answers

Using the charts as a guide, try creating verbs in different tenses in the sentences below.   Also translate the sentence. (Note: I have given you the root, definition, conjugation and tense.   It's up to you to figure out the proper form)

Lifnei chodesh ani **Tasti (טסתי)** (Tas (fly, past tense) li Tel-Aviv.   — **I flew to Tel Aviv a month ago.**

2.   Atah **Telech (תלך)** (Halach, you, go, future tense) le'Misada machar? –-
Are you going to the restaurant tomorrow?

3. Anachnu **Shatinu (שתינו)** (Shatah, drink, we) mayim me'od karim. — **We drank very cold water.**

4.   Mi **Shachach (שכח)**   (Shachach, forgot, past tense) darkon shelahem bamatos? — **Who forgot their passport on the airplane?**

5. Ani **Lomed (לומד)** (lamad, learn, present, I) Sefaradit veTzarfartit ba-Universita.
— **I study Spanish and French in College (University).**

Create a chart of your own for the verb *Lavash,* to wear, for past, present and future tenses.

Past Tense

Person	Masculine	Feminine
1st	Lavashti	Lavashti
2nd	Lavashta	Lavasht
3rd	Lavash	Lavsha
1st Plural	Lavashnu	Lavashnu
2nd Plural	Lavashtem	Lavashten
3rd Plural	Lavshu	Lavshu

Present Tense

Person	Masculine	Feminine
1st	Lovesh	Loveshet
2nd	Lovesh	Loveshet
3rd	Lovesh	Loveshet
1st Plural	Lovshim	Lovshot
2nd Plural	Lovshim	Lovshot
3rd Plural	Lovshim	Lovshot

Future Tense

Person	Masculine	Feminine
1st	Elbosh	Elbosh
2nd	Tibosh	Tilbishi
3rd	Yilbosh	Tilbosh
1st Plural	Nilbosh	Nilbosh
2nd Plural	Tilbishu	Tilbashna
3rd Plural	Yilbishu	Yilbishu

Chapter 20
Conjunctions and Other Random Words

This final chapter simply has a list of conjunctions and other useful words that will help you speak clear Hebrew. These include such as *Between,* and *That*. Below is a list of useful words I did not cover previously. Again, like usual, the word appears in Hebrew together with the transliteration.

Word	Translation
Beyn (בין)	Between
Asher/She- (ש/אשר–)	That
Im (עם)	With
Im (אם)	If (note the difference in spelling)
Efshar, Efshari (אפשרי)	Possible
Al (אל)	Don't
El (אל)	To (note the different pronunciation)
Bishvil (בשביל)	For
Lema'an (למען)	For the sake of, For
Ka-Asher/Ke-She (כאשר, כש–)	When (Not question)

Another thing to keep in mind with Hebrew is the use of affixes. As I've said before, you can add affixes to words that mean an entire word in English or another language and be able to create phrases solely with affixes and a single verb. Sometimes, this can even be a whole sentence. The examples used earlier in the book demonstrate this.

Note: This is especially common in the media, especially in news broadcasts on the radio and television. It also appears in the written word. However, in regards to the spoken word, Israelis do this. Immigrants however, usually have a hard time with this. Don't worry though. It takes time, but it is possible to learn all of the affixes and their usage.

Hazara!

Translate the following paragraph.   Feel free to use a dictionary as help.

Lifnei shlosha shavuot, hitchil matzav me'od mafchid.   Irgun terror echad hitchil lirot tilim al kol midinat Yisrael.   Yesh azakot bekol sha'ot ha yom.   BaShabbat yaru tilim beshesh baboker.   Az hamedina hitchil lehagen al atzmo ve'ezrachav veshalach hachail ha'avir tifkof kol makom shemimenu yatzah til.   Zeh hefchlif lifnei shavua lemilchama.   HaMivtza shekaru lo "Tzok Eitan" hu achehav "Milchemet Azza".   Ani lo yode'a ech zeh yistayeym aval ani mikaveh sheyihyeh bimhirut.

(לפני שלושה שבועות התהיל מצב מאד מפחיד. אירגון טרור אהד התחיל לירות טילים על כל מדינת
ישראל. יש אזעקות בכל שעות היום. בשבת ירו טילים בשש בבוקר. אז התחיל המדינה להגן על עצמו
ואזרחיו ושלח החיל האויר לתקוף כל מקום שממנו יצא טיל. זה החליף לפני שבוע למלחמה. המבצע
שקראו לו איתן צוק לו אין יודע לו אני. עזה מלחמת עכשיו הוא יסתיים אבל אני מקווה שיהיה
במהירות.)

Chapter 20 Answers

Translate the following paragraph.   Feel free to use a dictionary as help.

Three weeks ago, a scary situation began.   A terror organization began shooting rockets at all of Israel.   Air raid sirens go off at all hours of the day.   On Saturday they shot rockets at 6am.   The state began to defend itself and sent the air force to attack all places where rockets were shot from.   This past week it became a war.   The operation called "Tzok Eitan" is now "The Aza war".   I don't know how this will end, but I hope it will be soon.

Conclusion

Go young Grasshopper, Embark on Your Journey to the West!

You're now ready to travel!   You've learned a large amount of material that should help you get around Israel.   Obviously, you don't know everything, but you have a great foundation. Don't forget what you've learned!   Use the tools given at the beginning off the book, they will be your greatest asset when getting around Israel.   Use circumlocution, as people to repeat themselves if you must. You'll get the answer!

Be confident using your Hebrew.   Israelis appreciate the effort you make trying to speak their language.   They're more than willing to help you improve your Hebrew and will tell you when you make a mistake.   Speak to everyone you see on the street, Israelis love to talk about learn about other people and cultures.

To improve your Hebrew, focus on what was mentioned in the introduction. Surround yourself with the language.   Focus on learning to read Hebrew in the Hebrew script.   You could enroll in an *Ulpan*, the crash course in Hebrew given to immigrants to Israel that has now spread around the world as the most popular way to learn Hebrew.   You can find these programs in any Jewish community.   I highly recommend listening to Israeli radio an watching Israeli television if you can - you'll get an ear for the language and learn more vocabulary that way than you will in any book.   Plus, it's entertaining!

Don't worry about looking silly and just do your best to learn from the mistakes you make! I hope this book was helpful and that you have an exciting trip or trips to Israel!

To your success,

Dagny Taggart

Preview Of "Learn French In 7 DAYS! - The Ultimate Crash Course on Learning The Basics of the French Language In No Time"

Introduction

Why should YOU learn French?

Backpacking in the South of France? Dating a dreamy French man or a beautiful French lady? Planning a business meeting with French clients? Moving to a French-speaking country? Willing to show off at the next French festival of your local town?...

This book is for ALL OF YOU!

Thanks to this book, you'll get a grasp of what is French and how to master it! This book will offer you a complete overview of   the language along with useful expressions to start speaking.

French is a difficult language to learn... that's why this book makes it fun and easy... without forgetting efficiency!

By the end of this course, you will get the amazing feeling that YOU CAN DO IT! YOU CAN SPEAK FRENCH!

How will YOU learn French within a few weeks?

Are you aware that as an English speaker, you already know some 15,000 French words. The English language has indeed been shaped by many other languages, such as Latin, German, French.

The French influence on English dates back to the Norman invasion of England in 1066. It had a major impact not only on the country but on the language itself. William the Conqueror brought Norman French which became the language of the court, the government and the upper class for the next three centuries. During the Norman occupation, around 10,000 French words were adopted into English, of which about 75% are still used today. More than 30% of all English words are derived directly or indirectly from French.

If that doesn't convince you to learn French, the idea of visiting one of the 33 French-speaking countries over the world might do it!

French and English are the only languages spoken as a native language on 5 continents and the only languages taught in every country in the world. French is the official or one of the official languages in 33 countries[1]. This number is second to English, which is officially spoken in 45 countries.

Let's not wait anymore and indulge yourself in our learning program... and most of all, ENJOY every bit of the journey!

Chapter 1 : Introducing French

What you're about to learn:

    How to use French words you already know
    How to be at ease with French pronounciation

French/English similarities

The Normans brought French into the English language which resulted in more than 30% of French words currently being used by English natives. You may not be aware of it but everyday... you speak French!

Many of the words of French origin used in English find their roots in Latin and/or Greek. As an example, "beef" from French "boeuf" is meat from a cow

---

1   French is the official language of France and its overseas territories (French Guyana, Guadeloupe, Martinique, Mayotte, La Réunion, French Polynesia, New Caledonia, Saint Barts, Saint Martin, Saint Pierre and Miquelon, Wallis and Futuna) as well as 14 other countries: Bénin, Burkina Faso, Central African Republic, Democratic Republic of Congo, Republic of Congo, Côte d'Ivoire, Gabon, Guinea, Luxembourg, Mali, Monaco, Niger, Sénégal, Togo.

    French is also one of the official languages in the following countries: Belgium, Burundi, Cameroon, Canada, Chad, Channel Islands (Guernsey and Jersey), Comoros, Djibouti, Equatorial, Guinea, Haiti (the other official language is French Creole), Madagascar, Rwanda, Seychelles, Switzerland, Vanuatu.

(from old English "cu") which is a type of "bovine" from Latin "bovinus" via French "bovin".

For a clearer comprehension of the similarities, we have divided this paragraph into four different aspects related to the French influence in English language. There are original French words and expressions to be found in English, true cognates ("vrais amis"), false cognates ("faux amis") and spelling equivalents.

This will make it easier to understand how to use French words you already know and use in English!

French words & expressions in English

Over the years, an important number of French words and expressions have been absorbed by the English language and are still intact. Many English speakers might not even realize that they are using these French words in everyday conversations.

Some other words and expressions have been kept to add *a certain touch of French* – "un certain je ne sais quoi". English speakers seem to be aware of this French influence and intentionally using those words with a somewhat accurate pronunciation!

Below is a list of some common examples of French words and expressions used in English.

"adieu" : farewell
"à la carte" : on the menu
"à la mode" : in fashion/style (in English "with ice-cream")
"art déco" : decorative art
"au pair" : a person who works for a family in exchange for room and board
"avant-garde" : innovative (arts)
"brunette" : small, dark-haired female
"cordon bleu" : master chef
"coup d'état" : government overthrow
"cuisine" : type of food/cooking
"débutante" : beginner (In French, "débutante" is the feminine form of "débutant" which means in English beginner (noun) or beginning (adj). In both languages, it refers to a young girl making her formal début into society. Interestingly this usage is not original in French. It was adopted back from English.)

"déjà-vu" : feeling like you've already seen or done something
"haute couture" : high-class clothing style
"Mardi Gras" : Shrove Tuesday
"pot-pourri" : cented mixture of dried flowers and spices
"prêt-à-porter" : clothing
"savoir-faire" : know-how
"savoir-vivre" : manners, etiquette
"souvenir" : memento
"Bon appétit!" : Enjoy your meal!
"Bon voyage!" : Have a good trip!
"C'est la vie!" : That's life!
"Oh là là!" : Ooh la la!
"RSVP" ("Répondez s'il vous plaît") : Please RSVP
"Touché!" : You got me!
"Voilà!" : There it is!

True cognates ("vrais amis")

True cognates (true friends) are words with identical spelling and meaning in both French and English. Given the great use of these words in English, you already have a considerable asset to start using French vocabulary!

True cognates are pronounced differently most of the time. However the exact spelling makes it a great advantage to learn French as an English speaker. You can easily learn some French phrases that have several true cognates.

For instance, "je vais voir un film au cinéma ce week-end avec mon cousin" can be understood with the words "film", "cinema", "weekend" and "cousin". You can easily come up with a translation thanks to the French cognates: "I will go to the movies this weekend with my cousin".

Note: "cousin" is used in both French and English to refer to the son (or daughter in English) of one of your sibling. While it remains the same for male and female in English, the feminine form has a different spelling in French: "cousine".

Did you really think that it was so hard to speak French? Just start using the hundreds of words you already use everyday!
The list of French cognates is incredibly long – they are estimated to be some 1,700 words! The following list is just a sample of some of the most common true cognates used in English.

Useful to learn French:

"accent" (masculine noun)
"alphabet" (masculine)

Useful words at work:

"absence" (feminine noun)
"accident" (masculine)
"client" (masculine)
"collaboration" (feminine)
"communication" (feminine)
"contact" (masculine)
"document" (masculine)
"fax" (masculine)
"message" (masculine)
"mission" (feminine)
"obligation" (feminine)
"payable" (adjective)
"profession" (feminine)
"solution" (feminine)
"test" (masculine)

Planning your weekend get-away:

"barbecue" (masculine)
"bikini" (masculine)
"bistro" (masculine)
"bungalow" (masculine)
"camp" (masculine)
"casino" (masculine)
"concert" (masculine)
"kayak" (masculine noun)
"parachute" (masculine)
"parasol" (masculine)
"promenade" (feminine)
"ski" (masculine)
"sport" (masculine)
"taxi" (masculine)

"tennis" (masculine)
"valise" (feminine)
"zoo" (masculine)

At the restaurant:

"addition" (feminine)
"apéritif" (masculine)
"chef" (masculine)
"dessert" (masculine)
"entrée" (feminine)
"fruit" (masculine)
"gourmet" (masculine)
"hors-d'oeuvre" (masculine)
"menu" (masculine)
"pizza" (feminine)
"quiche" (feminine)
"sorbet" (masculine)
"steak" (masculine)
"vodka" (feminine)

False cognates ("faux-amis")

In French, there are numerous "faux-amis" (false cognates or false friends). These words can cause communication problems as they look alike in French and English but have a totally different meaning.

A wrong use of a false friend can end up by a funny joke or a lack of respect. As an example, it can be funny to hear that someone never buys food containing "préservatifs", which in French means "condoms"! However it would not be clever to mistake "pain", which means "bread" in French, with the actual English word (the correct French word being "douleur"). You never know what you will end up getting at the drugstore!

Here is a list of the most common "faux-amis" to avoid stupid mistakes that will haunt you forever!

French faux ami	English translation
actuel	Current, present

actuellement	Currently, presently
agenda	diary
allure	pace, appearance, style
assister à	to attend
attendre	to wait
avertissement	warning
balance	scale
blesser	to wound
bribes	fragments
car	coach
cave	cellar
chair	flesh
chance	luck
coin	corner
déception	disappointment
demander	to ask for
éventuellement	possibly
fabrique	factory
formidable	terrific
génial	brilliant
gentil	kind
injures	insult
lecture	reading
nouvelle	piece of news, short story
patron	boss
préservatif	condom
procès	trial
prune	plum
quitter	to leave
rester	to stay
sensible	sensitive
tissu	fabric

"Franglais" refers to the massive invasion of French by English words and expressions thanks to the globalization, bringing a worldwide popular culture, and the access to the internet. It has become trendy to use English words in French language. Despite many efforts, the French have failed into translating these English words in their own language, unlike the Canadian French who remarkably succeed in finding equivalents for every English word!

Below is a short list of the most common English words used by French speakers:

baby-foot	table football
basket	Sports shoe, basketball
brushing	blow-dry
camping	campsite
dressing	walk-in closet
catch	wrestling
flipper	pinball machine
footing	jogging
forcing	pressure
jogging	tracksuit
lifting	face-lift
people	celebrity
planning	schedule
pressing	dry-cleaner
relooking	make-over
smoking	tuxedo
sweat	sweatshirt
warning	hazard lights

Pronunciation

The French alphabet has the same number of letters as the English one. There are 6 vowels ("une voyelle") and 20 consonants ("une consonne").

A **vowel** is a sound that is pronounced through the mouth (or the nose for nasal vowels) with no obstruction of the lips, tongue, or throat.

There are a few general guidelines to keep in mind when pronouncing French vowels:

Most French vowels are pronounced further forward in the mouth than their English counterparts.

The tongue must remain tensed throughout the pronunciation of the vowel.

As for the **consonants**, many of them are similar in French and English so they should be quite easy to learn.

As an approach to French pronunciation ("la prononciation"), we propose you to use the following guide throughout the chapters.

Always refer to this pronunciation guide whenever you try to say a French word from our book. You can also complement your studies with vocal guides to be easily found on the Internet.

Simple letters **("les lettres simples"):**

French letters	Sounds like	English examples	French examples
a	a	r[a]t	bras (arm), chat (cat)
b	b	[b]utter	bateau (boat), bébé (baby)
c before o,a,u	k	[c]andy	carte (map), col (collar)
c before e,i,y	s	[s]tanza	citron (lemon), ciment (cement)
ç	s	[s]ilence	ça (this), garçon (boy)
d	d	[d]og	dos (back), dans (in)
e	u	b[u]bble	le (the), ce (this)
f	f	[f]lood	faire (to make), fleur (flower)
g before o,a,u	g	[g]row	gauche (left), guerre

			(war)
g before e,i,y	j	dé[j]à vu	orange (orange), girafe (giraffe)
h always silent	–	–	hibou (owl), hache (ax)
i	ee	f[ee]t	bisou (kiss), cri (shout)
j	j	dé[j]à vu	je (I), jamais (never)
k	k	[k]oala	képi (kepi), koala (koala)
l	l	[l]ove	lapin (rabbit), livre (book)
m	m	[m]other	maman (mom), mon (mine)
n	n	[n]ever	non (no), nid (nest)
o	o	z[o]rro	domino (domino), collègue (colleague)
p	p	[p]asta	papa (dad), patate (potatoe)
q	q	[c]ap	quatre (four), qui (who)
r	r	a[r]t deco	rare (unsual), radis (radish)
s	s	[s]nail	son (sound), savoir (know)
t	t	[t]ag	tata (auntie), ton (your)
u	ew	déjà v[u]	tu (you), ruban (ribbon)
v	v	[v]iew	vivre (to live), venir (to come)

w	v	wa[v]e	wagon
w (English origin)	w	[w]ater	whisky, wapiti
x inside a word or when ex- is followed by a consonnant or at the end of words	x	e[x]cess	expert, luxe (luxury)
x at the begining of a word or when ex- is followed by a vowel or h	x	e[x]am	exemple (example), examen (exam, test)
x at the end of words	s	[s]olution	dix (ten), six (six)
x (rare cases)	z	[z]ero	deuxième (second)
x at the end of words to indicate plural	silent	–	choux (cabbages), chevaux (horses)
y	y	[y]am	yoyo, yacht
z	z	[z]ip	zéro (zero), zèbre (zebra)

- **Complex sounds ("les sons complexes"):**

French sounds	Sounds like	English examples	French examples
ai	ai	l[ai]ssez-faire	aimer (to love), faire (to do)
-ain, -aim	un	Verd[un]	pain (bread), faim (hunger)
au	o	r[o]pe	paume (palm), baume (balm)
ch	sh	[sh]ampoo	château (castle), chapeau (hat)
ei	e	m[e]n	peine (pain), reine (queen)
eu	e	th[e]	peu (little), deux (two)

French letters	Sounds like	English examples	French examples
-er, -ez	a	d[a]y	manger (to eat), vous allez (you go)
eau, -aud, -ot	o	[o]zone	rateau (rake), chaud (hot), pot (jar)
em, en before consonant	en	[en]core	entre (between), emploi (job)
ha-	a	r[a]t	habiter (to live)
ill	y	[y]ogurt	fille (girl), billet (ticket)
oi	wa	[wa]ter	toit (roof), quoi (what)
oin	oo + un	t[oo]+Verd[un]	loin (far), coin (corner)
on, om	on	s[on]g	bon (good), chanson (song)
ou	oo	t[wo]	fou (crazy), cou (neck)
ph	f	[f]ather	phare (lighthouse)
sc before o,a,u	sc	[sc]oundrel	sculpter (to sculpt), scorpion
sc before e,i,y	sc	[sc]enario	scie (saw), scène (stage)
th	t	[t]ime	thym (thyme), thèse (thesis)
ti	s	[s]tone	objection (objection), prophétie (prophecy)
um, un word ending or before a consonant	un	Verd[un]	un (a), parfum (perfume)
ui	wi	ki[wi]	pluie (rain), cuisine (kitchen)

- **Accents ("les accents")**

French letters	Sounds like	English examples	French examples
à	a	r[a]t	à (in)

é	a	d[a]y	école (school), café (coffee)
è, ê	e	m[e]n	père (father), mère (mother)
â,î,ô,û pronounced as a,i,o,u			château (castle), hôpital (hospital) ...
ä, ë, ï, ö, ü the tréma indicates that the two adjacent vowels must both be pronounced	a i	n[a i]ve	Noël (Christmas), haïr (to hate)

"Test your French!"

Let's review what you've learnt in that chapter with a few exercises.

Mark the correct answers:

In French, "people" is used to mean:
☐ a young person
☐ an old person
☐ a celebrity

In English, "brilliant" is the translation of the following French word:
☐ brilliant
☐ épatant
☐ génial

In French, "brunette" refers to :
☐ a type of food
☐ a small, dark-haired female
☐ a painting color

Which of the following words is a true cognate (true friend)?"
☐ actually
☐ car
☐ pot-pourri

Which of the following is a false cognate (false friend)?

□ préservatif
□ débutante
□ gourmet

Which of the following English term uses the French sound "eau" like in "chapeau" (hat)?
□ face
□ throw
□ shampoo

Which of the following English term uses the French sound "ai" like in "aimer" (to love)?
□ well
□ parade
□ three

Answers:

In French, "people" is used to mean:
□ a celebrity

In English, "brilliant" is the translation of the following French word:
□ génial

In French, "brunette" refers to :
□ a small, dark-haired female

Which of the following words is a true cognate (true friend)?"
□ pot-pourri

Which of the following is a false cognate (false friend)?
□ préservatif

Which of the following English term uses the French sound "eau" like in "chapeau" (hat)?
□ throw

Which of the following English term uses the French sound "ai" like in "aimer" (to love)?
□ well

To check out the rest of "Learn French In 7 DAYS! - The Ultimate Crash Course on Learning The Basics of the French Language In No Time" go to Amazon and look for it right now!

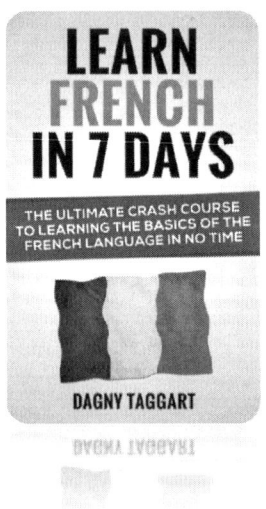

Ps: You'll find many more books like these under my name, Dagny Taggart. Don't miss them! Here's a short list:

- Learn **Spanish** In 7 Days!
- Learn **French** In 7 Days!
- Learn **German** In 7 Days!
- Learn **Italian** In 7 Days!
- Learn **Portuguese** In 7 Days!

- Learn **Japanese** In 7 Days!
- Learn **Chinese** In 7 Days!

- Learn **Russian** In 7 Days!

- Learn Any Language FAST!

- How to Drop Everything & Travel Around The World

About the Author

Dagny Taggart is a language enthusiast and polyglot who travels the world, inevitably picking up more and more languages along the way.

 Taggart's true passion became learning languages after she realized the incredible connections with people that it fostered. Now she just can't get enough of it. Although it's taken time, she has acquired vast knowledge on the best and fastest ways to learn languages. But the truth is, she is driven simply by her motive to build exceptional links and bonds with others.

She is inspired everyday by the individuals she meets across the globe. For her, there's simply not anything as rewarding as practicing languages with others because she gets to make friends with people from all that come from a variety of cultures. This, in turn, has broadened her mind and thinking more than she would have ever imagined it could.

Of course, as a result of her constant travels, Taggart has become an expert on planning trips and making the most of time spent out of what she calls her "base" town. She jokes that she's practically at the nomad status now, but she's more content to live that way.

She knows how to live on a manageable budget weather she's in Paris or Phnom Penh. She knows how to seek out the adventures and thrills, no doubt, lying in wait at any city she visits. She knows that reflection on each every experience is significant if she wants to grow as a traveler and student of the world's cultures.

Because of this, Taggart chooses to share her understanding of languages and travel so that others, too, can experience the same life-altering benefits she has.

Printed in Great Britain
by Amazon.co.uk, Ltd.,
Marston Gate.